To   Auntie Belle & Uncle Bill,

A Picture of Prague, where I (Ailsa) have
been working for the last two years,

Love + Best Wishes,
Ailsa & Peter

X X,

PRAGUE

A WALK THROUGH
HISTORY

Prague

A WALK THROUGH
HISTORY

MARIE VITOCHOVÁ
JINDŘICH KEJŘ

JIŘÍ & IVAN DOLEŽAL

V RÁJI

Working over the text of the book we applied
own conclusions of ours, relying upon
the valuable information from the works
of the following authors:
Marie Bláhová, Jiří Burian, Petr Čornej, Zdeněk Dragoun,
Tomáš Durdík, František Ekert, Michal Flegl, Ivan Hlaváček,
Václav Hlavsa, Jaromír Homolka, Petr Chotěbor, Josef Janáček,
František Kašička, Božena Kopičková, Dobroslav Líbal, Vilém Lorenc,
Josef Mayer, Dobroslava Menclová, Bořivoj Nechvátal,
Helena Olmerová, Emanuel Poche, Ctibor Rybár, Jiří Spěváček,
Jaroslava Staňková, Karel Stejskal, František Šmahel, Jiří Štursa,
V. V. Tomek, Jiří Vančura, Milada Vilímková,
Pavel Vlček, Svatopluk Voděra, Vojtěch Volavka, Zdeněk Wirth

ISBN 80–900875–3–1

PRAGUE,
THE MOTHER OF TOWNS

I n the very heart of Bohemia (Čechy) lies Prague (Praha). The city was predestined for a metropolis by just its advantageous geographical position in the basin through which the Vltava River flows in its meandrous bed. Prague grew during long centuries from the settlements which clustered gradually below the two castles standing on the elevations above the Vltava – the older, Prague Castle (Pražský hrad), and the newer, Vyšehrad. The old dynastic legend connects the foundation of the Town of Prague with the presence of

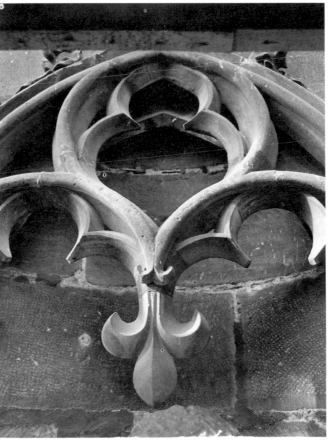

Libuše, the mythical Czech Princess and Prophetess. It is said that when the Princess called on Přemysl, a ploughman whom she chose as her consort, to the Princely Throne, the foundation of Prague was foretold with her words, "Town, I can see, large, whose glory touches the stars." That event of still the olden pagan times, sometime short after the settlement of the land by the Czech Slavs, became, together with the cult of the later Přemyslid St. Wenceslaw (sv. Václav, † 935), one of the pillars of the medieval state and dynastic tradition.

However, in reality the foundation of Prague Castle occurred after 880, when the first historically documented Přemyslid, Bořivoj ("Who Destroys Guards"), having been baptized, transferred the Princely Seat from the not very distant and north located Levý Hradec–on––Vltava here, on the headland above the bend of the Vltava, where he built his stronghold and its church consecrated to Our Lady. Soon below the new stronghold, on the slopes and also in the fluvial plain of the Vltava, lay villages and fishermen's settlements, and originated marketplaces with goods both domestic and offered by foreign traders whose caravans came frequently along this trail. Under the protection by the Princely Castle the foreign traders stopped here not only for trade reasons, but also for having a rest before futher traveling.

The importance of Prague as a center of unified Bohemia grew at the end of the 10th century. Bohemia was then visited by Ibrahim Ibn Jacob, a Jewish merchant from Tortosa (a place on the Iberian Peninsula), who, in his book of travel and for the first time, depicts Prague as an architecturally rich seat of Dukedom, and described also the settlement around the Castle as an important stopping–place for long–distance business routes.

During the 10th century, the other princely castle, Vyšehrad, was built on the south side of the Vltava basin. Vyšehrad was mistaken as older than Prague Castle in the later tradition; it is, however, just the Vyšehrad Rock which is connected with the legend of Princess Libuše and her prophecies.

During the further two centuries, settlements and their marketplaces formed in the space between the two Castles. The new settlements were often the enlargements to older settled places. The importance, wealth and architectural richness of those settlements (then still called Mezihradí, i. e. "Between Castles") grew and this meant the urban bases were originating for the ensuing towns of Prague.

A look in the presbytery of the Church of St. Saviour (kostel sv. Salvatora) in the complex of St. Agnes of Bohemia's Convent (sv. Anežka Česká) from the 13th century

Prague in the Late Romanesque period was already a large settlement of urban type, with marketplaces, stone churches and the first convents, and with ostentatious merchant houses and nobles' seats. The larger and more important settlement was being created in the broad and shallow rightbank part of the Vltava's basin. Communication with the Duke's Castle and with the settlements below the Castle was provided by at first wooden and later stone Judithy Bridge. The process of transforming the urban–type settlements along both banks of the Vltava into actual towns was completed only by the construction of walls. The Walls were a matter not only

From the Lesser Town Bishop's Palace, built during the time
of John IV of Dražice, the Early Gothic tower has only
remained up to the present time

The Bethlehem Chapel (Betlémská kaple) from the end
of the 14th century, the place of sermons preached
by Master John Hus

of military defense character. They were also confirming the successfulness of the process of municipal area unification, and they were creating the prerequisites to the development of collective urban life style.

The stately development of Prague in the reign of the last Přemyslid kings was undoubtedly connected with their growing power, and therefore, with the importance of the Czech State in the Central European region. The Castle becomes a grandiose royal seat, the policy-and--power center of the Czech State. The Castle's requirements influenced the economic development of Prague as favorably as the increase in population which was allowed by the continuing capability to complete the settlement in vacant areas on the defined municipal land.

A positive influence was shown also by the discovery of the rich deposits of Czech silver, whose stimulating influence showed in the political and economic development throughout the Kingdom and naturally, first of all this source of wealth showed in the development of Prague, which was the most important economic center of the land.

E ven in the political struggles and disorders in the early 14th century, which brought Prague and their inhabitant nothing else than sufferings and material losses, at last the economic development of Prague weakened not very much. The growing wealthiness of burghers manifested itself outwards in the growing material culture of everyday life. First of all in the houses of merchants and better–off craftsmen, though the burghers' practicalness only exerted an influence upon the slow change in the methods of construction, which already accepted the new, Gothic style, the style which was used much earlier and more in the construction of new buildings of sacral nature. With the growing abundance and self–confidence of burghers, growing were also the burghers' political demands, and namely first of all in the reign of Wenceslas II; however, the burghers' aspirations found their satisfaction no sooner than in the reign of John of Luxemburg (Jan Lucemburský), when finally the aldermen succeeded in obtaining the writ allowing to establish the Town Hall as a seat of Self–Government for the Town of Prague.

Prague, during its thousand years' development, came in for a number of celebrative attributes praising its beauty, architectural richness and largeness, and Prague was once called Golden after the gilt roofs over the gates of Prague Castle, once the Hundred–Spired after the countless number of towers and spires of various shapes and the most diversified decorative elements protruding above the sea of roofs on Prague houses. Prague then already was undergoing the great reconstruction and substantial enlargement in the reign of Charles IV (Karel IV.), who had made a resolution to make the conurbation and both Castles not only a dignified metropolis for the Lands of the Czech Crown, but also for the entire Holy Roman Empire, whose King of the Romans and, at a later time, Emperor, he became.

T hough short after the death of King Charles IV Prague lost its importance as the seat of the mightiest ruler of the then Christian world, as Charles' son Wenceslas IV was removed from the Throne of Rome and in the ensuing historic stage, the Hussite Revolution – the curtain raiser to the great European revolutions –, it was on the other hand the Praguers themselves and their political representation who exercised, perfectly and from the very beginning of the Revolution, the municipal economic and military potential, and with the help of their countryside allies they played a role which extended far beyond the borders of the then Kingdom of Bohemia. The Calix was not a mere symbol of the victorious Revolution, but it became at the end of the Revolution an actual result, recognized even by the highest institute of Church then, the Council. Prague was then the actual center and recognized heart of the Czech Lands, which was respected by both domestic allies and the foreign or domestic enemies as well.

Prague even in the kingless period before the mid–15th century retained its position, and moreover, the Council Hall at the Old Town Hall became then the place where not seldom the destinies of the entire Kingdom were decided upon. And therefore it did not happen by a chance that the high political prestige of Praguers was further confirmed at the Old Town Hall by the election of a new King from the rank of domestic noblemen, the George of Poděbrady (Jiří z Poděbrad), who took the Imperial Throne to become a just King (1458–1471) for the people of two denominations – for Catholics and Calixtins.

After the reign of George of Poděbrady, famous inter alia for his peacemaking initiative with which he applied to the then rulers of the Christian World, it was the rulers of the Polish Jagiello dynasty who took their turns. During their reigns the picture of Gothic Prague and Prague Castle was being completed with the real gems of Late Gothic architecture. However, in that period Prague lost its shine of the Royal Seat, because King Vladislav Jagiello (Vladislav Jagellonský), after he became also King of Hungary, transferred his seat to Buda, as he obliged himself to do this before the Buda Estates already during the Election Act. In domestic political disputes with aristocracy, Prague as the leader of Royal Towns was a consistent advocate of the validity of its Third Vote at the Assemblies of Estates. The right to Third Vote was confirmed to the Towns in 1508, and the disputes between the Noblemen's Estates and Knights' Estates as one party and the Town Union as the other party (represented first of all by Prague) ended in the so–called St. Wenceslas Treaty in 1517.

T hat important act, though deciding by far not all the matters which constituted tensions in mutual relations between the parties to the dispute, assured partially the political and economic position of Prague and further Royal Towns, the position obtained already before. And it was nothing earlier than the disastrous participation of Praguers in the 1st Rising of Estates in 1547 against Ferdinand I, what allowed the victorious Monarch to fully get under control Prague, the city which, with respect to its political authority and economic power and over many decades, was accustomed to behave in much sovereign way in the framework

of the Kingdom. The institution of King's Magistrates and Administrators meant that the Municipal Self–Government became fully dependent upon those officers appointed by the King and coming from the rank of aristocracy. The Prague Old Town Hall, the political head of the Town Estates, thus became a subordinate body without an actual opportunity of pursuing an independent policy.

At the close of the 16th century in the reign of the Emperor Rudolph II the former Imperial Seat shine of Prague revived, as the Emperor, in whose reign the Renaissance stage of Prague's reconstruction was being completed, was also a keen admirer and sponsor of art. And therefore at his Court in Prague, beside political personalities who were sent as negotiators to Prague from Royal Courts of the whole of Europe, appeared also painters, sculptors, musicians, men of letters, astrologers and, naturally, alchemists, from all parts, because at Rudolph's Court everybody enjoyed the interest showed by the educated Emperor and simultaneously everybody was given material security.

H owever, then in Bohemia a conflict was gradually approaching of power and religion, which burst out in full in 1618, through several times diverted by diplomatic activities of both parties. The consequences of that conflict were far reaching, they exceeded the framework of Prague and Kingdom of Bohemia and threw the then powers of Europe in the war rage lasting thirty years. The dangerous flames of that fire flared up on May 23, 1618 in Prague, when the Protestant Czech Estates issued, through the throwing (i. e. Defenestration) of Royal Governors out of the windows of the so–called Louis Wing in the Royal Palace in Prague Castle, the command to commence the 2nd Rising of Estates. However the whole revolt against the Habsburgs ended, as inglorious, two years later in the lost battle of the White Mountain (Bílá hora), followed by: the panic getaway of Frederick of the Palatinate (Fridrich Falcký) called the Winter King after his reign long a mere winter; the executions of leaders of revolting Estates on the Old Town Square (the repre-

The Loretto courtyard and the Church of the Nativity (kostel Narození Páně), and the Holy House – a copy of the original pilgrimage place in Loretto in Italy

View through the Romanesque arcade of the Strahov Premonstratensian Order's Monastery (Strahovský klášter), founded by the second Czech King Vladislav I

The entrance part of Černín Palace on Loretto Square (Loretánské náměstí) from the second half of the 17th century, when the Palace was built at the building expenses of John Černín of Chudenice; today, the Federal Ministry of Foreign Affairs

sentatives of Towns of Prague were among those executed); the forced recatholicization of most inhabitants; and the first collective Bohemian and Moravian Exodus in whose crowds were such great personages as John Amos Comenius (Jan Ámos Komenský). A number of Praguers were fined for their, though mostly passive, part in the revolt, and thousands of people preferred leaving the country to giving up their faith. The severest consequence, however, of the White Mountain disaster to the City was the economic and political decay.

In the subsequent period the Czech Capital became a mere provincial town in the Habsburg Empire, and the destructive Thirty Years' War, which touched Prague directly for several times, only completed the process of the political and economic decline of Prague.

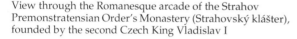

he mentioned development was seemingly in an absolute contradiction to the rapid renewal of building activities, which was caused by the need to fortify, anew and thoroughly and fully to the spirit already of the Baroque fortress building style, the Towns of Prague and the two Castles as well, the need was proved by the unfortunate experiences of the past war years. A contribution to the revival of building activities in Prague was also shown by the large–scale seizures of the possessions of non––Catholics, which laid foundations, both areal and financial, for the erection of large church complexes and the new aristocratic buildings of the White Mountain victors' families. the Baroque soon after the end of the Thirty Years' War gained gradually Prague, whose nature was still

Roofs of the Lesser Town palaces

the medieval one in spite of the Renaissance paint, and Prague was step by step changed into a Baroque city with the lovely architectural dominants along both banks of the Vltava.

The substantial change, which was introduced in Prague by the Baroque architecture, was a unification: the Baroque gave the city the new, architecturally consistent appearance. New palaces were built up and decorative gardens were conceived, and in accordance with the newest experience of fortification engineering of that time, the bastion fortifications originated in the New Town and the Lesser Town, and Vyšehrad, Prague Castle and Hradčany as well. Reconstructed or entirely new built were churches, hospitals and of Prague burghers, including their properties beyond the City Walls. Some of the buildings have survived up to the present. Both Castles underwent substantial building modifications. While Vyšehrad was transformed, gradually and to the intentions of the State, into a mighty Baroque Fortress which defended the City from the south, Prague Castle underwent a grandiose Baroque completion, which reached its height in the reign of Maria Theresa already in the Classicistic era.

The Rococo and Classicistic styles completed the changeover of Medieval Prague. The bulk of building activities became the fulfilling of orders of nouveaux riches, and it was their possessions on which the changeover of Prague into a picturesque and peaceful seat occurred.

The Baroque copulas and domes on houses and towers, the mansards, gables and dormers, the Rococo or Classicistic facades down in the City, and above, the coulisse of the Classicist frontages of the Palaces in Prague Castle, they gave Prague and its panorama the entirely new impression.

Within the Walls of Prague the medieval way of living preserved nearly to the end of the 18th century. The lifestyle was hit in a pervasive manner no earlier than by the economic and social changes in the reign of Joseph II.

In 1784 the Towns of Prague – Old Town, New Town, Lesser Town, and Hradčany – were united in one entity with one common Municipal Council. The Enlightened Emperor considered in his reform policy the Prague Ghetto, whose me-

dieval separation was abolished by his decree. However the Jewish Town, called Josefov, reached its full emancipation no earlier than in 1850, when Josefov was proclaimed the fifth district of Prague. In 1883 the City was given the sixth district, Vyšehrad. In the following years the modern Prague agglomeration developed at a pace actually dizzying.

After the War of 1866 between Prussia and Austria it showed that the large Baroque fortifications, following basically the strip of medieval Walls of New Town and Old Town, were useless from a military point of view, and moreover, that the fortifications were a bar to an economic and building development of Prague. The demolition of the Walls occurred however only after 1871. Regardless of this, beyond the Walls line from the 1830s onwards the first industrial businesses have already grown, the number of inhabitants grew, and the former villages sprang up as new densely populated towns almost overnight.

The development in the industries was supported also by the introduction of railroad transport, local transit, horse streetcar lines, and, at the close of the century, electrical streetcar lines. The 19th century manifests itself outwards in a number of entirely new municipal constructions and in the complete new streets of burgher houses built in historicizing styles. After the Neo–Gothic, Neo–Renaissance and Late Classicism, also the Neo–Baroque comes in the streets of Prague, and mainly at the beginning of the 20th century, also the Sezession style comes in Prague. New parts of Prague have been already built in accordance with modern architectural criteria.

Prague became the Capital of the Czechoslovakian State. An Act of 1920 created Greater Prague, in whose union were incorporated the large suburbs which formerly had statutes of independent towns, together with tens of villages and settlements over a vast area. The period between the two World Wars meant a large increase in population, which brought a building boom. New residential and industrial entities grew on the outskirts of the City, family houses development flourished in the suburbs. The entrepreneurial spiriti connected with the architectural avant–garde hit also the City Center, though not always happy but in a number

An example of Prague Sezession – the Main Railroad Station
building, from the beginning of the 20th century

15

Sculptures of the portal of Clam–Gallas Palace by Matthias
Bernard Braun

of cases with remarkable implementations
of principal cultural importance.

The growing of Prague continued even after
the interruption by the Second World War and
the Nazi occupation. In the post–war period
the area of Prague was enlarged for three times
to reach the current area of 496 km^2, and in spite
of: a number of difficulties caused by neglecting
the proper care of certain vital functions; the insufficient facilities for citizen's needs in the new
dwelling districts and their "military barracks"
styles and their transport or transit problems,
Prague nowadays is ready to solve its environ-
mental and transport problems, problems
in the maintenance of the City proper, and
problems in the structure of services.

Much work and mainly the considerable financial means should be paid to the regeneration of
Prague's historical nucleus, whose substantial
part forms the City's Monument Reservation.
Moreover, the complex of Prague Castle is a special territory from the Monument Protection
viewpoint, and also a number of further monuments are given the highest degree of protection
as the National Cultural Monuments.

**The Prague of today is finally, after long
decades, a city in an independent state.
Prague is an open book of the historical
events both national and continental, and
generously offers its beautiful parts,
cultural gems and historical evidence
for learning.**

The National Theater (Národní divadlo) was built
in the "Nationals for One Another" manner
in the North Italian Late Renaissance style,
from plans by architect Joseph Zítek

17

The towers and domes of churches protrude above the roofs
of the Old Town houses

View of the Vltava River Bridges with the parts of Old Town
Mills and the gilt roof of the National Theater

19

Two symbols of Prague – the Monument to Master John Hus and the burgher Cathedral of Our Lady Before Týn (katedrála Panny Marie před Týnem) on the Old Town Square (Staroměstské náměstí)

A gem of the Prague Sezession – the Municipal Halls House (Obecní dům) from the beginning of the 20th century

The Carolinum – the oriel of the University Chapel.
The Chapel dates from the period after 1385

A single, slim octagonal tower, called the Prague Minaret,
has survived from the Gothic Church of St. Catherine
(kostel sv. Kateřiny) in the Upper New Town

PRAGUE CASTLE

From this Castle in future two golden olive trees will grow, whose tops will reach the Seventh Heaven, and all over the World they will shine with Signs and Miracles. They will be honored with offerings and presents by all the tribes of Bohemia and other peoples. One of them will be called Maior gloria (Major Glory), the other Exercitus consolatio (Consolation to the Guard). This will happen in future after a long time. Because the Glorious Prince of the Kingdom of Bohemia, the famous Martyr Wenceslas, which is pronounced Václav in the Slavonic language and translated Magna gloria (Great Glory), and the blessed Adalbert the Martyr, the second Bishop of Prague, whose name is translated Consolatio exercitus (Consolation to the Guard), came into blossom on the said Castle.

FROM THE PROPHECY BY PRINCESS LIBUŠE
IN THE CHRONICLE OF BOHEMIA
BY PŘIBÍK OF RADENÍN, CALLED PULKAVA

The Princely Stronghold, and later the Castle of Bohemian Kings, was founded on the headland which opens wide southwards in the Vltava Basin and is separated northwards with a deep valley through which the Brusnice Stream runs down to join the Vltava. The long shape of the headland, which descends on the east side to the river, reminded already the old Czechs of a dog's long spine and tail, or of a dolphin's body, and therefore such a comparison appears even in the oldest records by analecta keepers. On the west side, which was the least accessible, the path to the Stronghold was cut across with a broad dug moat spanned with a bridge, as recollected in 1004 by Cosmas, the oldest Czech chronicler.

The original Stronghold was founded probably sometime after 880 by the Czech Prince Bořivoj, who before, together with his consort Ludmila, was converted from the hands of Method (Metoděj), the Slavonic Apostle. At a later time Prince Bořivoj also founded in those parts the first Christian Church consecrated to Our Lady, whose foundation remnants stayed preserved.

Inside the Clementinum complex
is the Astronomical Tower from which orders were once
issued to fire a gun to announce the precise time

In the middle of the Stronghold stood the Princely Fort, east of which before 920 Prince Wratislaw founded the little Church of St. George (sv. Jiří), which was later reconstructed into a Romanesque Basilica with the Convent of Benedictines. Wratislaw's son Wenceslas (Václav) built, on the west side and also on the centerline of the Stronghold headland, the multi–story Rotunda, which was consecrated to St. Vitus (sv. Vít) – the future main Cathedral of Bohemia. After the establishment of the independent Bishopric in 973 (whose first Bishop was a Saxon, Dietmar) the Chapel of the Bishop was also built and consecrated to St. Maurice.

The personage of Prince Wenceslas is important for Prague Castle and for the history of the whole of Czech nation, because Wenceslas was the first Saint of Bohemia and Patron of the Land. However in 935 Wenceslas was murdered in a conspiracy of magnates on the Castle of his younger brother Boleslav, who had been instiated into the preparations of coup and murder. On the one hand, legends depict Prince Boleslav I as an active fratricide, on the other hand the legends mentioned his care over the dignified burial of Wenceslas' remains in St. Vitus Rotunda, in the place which was chosen by Wenceslas himself for his repose. Boleslav became successor to St. Wenceslas on the Princely Throne and changed foreign orientation of the Dukedom of Bohemia from Bavaria towards the Saxon dynasty. Christianization continued in Bohemia, and Boleslav's endeavor after the strengthening of canonical order was crowned in the reign of his son, Boleslav II, by establishing the Bishopric for Bohemia, which was however subordinated to the Archbishopric of Mainz. Short afterwards the praising started of Prince Wenceslas as Saint and Peacemaker, and later also as Patron of the Land and the mystical keeper of the Bohemian Reign, as that reign was only conferred upon living members of Přemyslids House and then upon their successors. From Wenceslas Rotunda preserved have been the mere remainders of masonry, mostly from the southern apse with the Saint's sepulchre in the area of today's St. Wenceslas Chapel (svatováclavská kaple) in the Cathedral into which over centuries the original modest Wenceslas' little Church changed.

Around 1050 Duke Břetislav I ordered to replace the rampart fortifications of Prague Castle with stone walls, and Duke Spytihněv II commenced, in 1060 and in the place where Wenceslas Rotunda stood, the construction of two–Chancel Basilica, consecrated to Saints Vitus, Wenceslas, and Adalbert (Vojtěch) and the Martyrs, and to Our Lady at the west end chancel. The construction of the Cathedral survived even a Castle fire and was completed around 1090 in the reign of Wratislaw, the first King of Bohemia. Then also the Monastery of the Prague Church was built as a seat of the Metropolitan Chapter, which was established as early as at the close of Millennium. The Chapter played its important role in culture and education (at the Chapter was a Latin School, the supreme domestic school before the establishment of Prague University) and in the development of the Czech State, which simply could not do without the administrative and diplomatic activities of educated persons of the Church. It was however just the King Wratislaw I, who tried to compensate the excessive influence of St. Vitus canonry with the establishment of the new, Vyšehrad Chapter. We are obliged to the St. Vitus Chapter even for the oldest preserved Chronicle of Bohemia from the pen of the educated and much–traveled Cosmas († 1125), who recorded both the older stories and messages and the authentic testimonies to the events which occurred in domestic or European environment during his long life.

In the 12th century Prague Castle underwent a very boisterous times, however in spite of the numerous peripeteia, the changing of rulers and war rages the insuppressible prosperity of the Land, and of the settlement below Prague Castle in particular, showed in the growth and architectural richness of the Castle, which were retained by the Castle basically until the mid–14th century. After 1135 Duke Soběslav I commenced the reconstruction of Prague Castle in a "metropolis Bohemiae Pragam more Latinorum civitatum colpit renovari" style, i. e. he started habilitating the main Castle in Bohemia after the mode of development of Romanesque cities west and south of the Bohemian border forests.

The west slim towers and the front of St. Vitus' Cathedral
(katedrála sv. Víta) date from the Cathedral's completion
at the end of the 19th century, as designed by Architect
Joseph Mocker

The entire periphery of the Castle fortifications was walled carefully in range masonry of white ashlar stones and equipped with the bastions, which are still discernable in the internal itemization as well as facades of the later Castle buildings, in particular on the south side and on the west side. Also the Princely Palace on the south border of the Castle was rebuilt into a large, representative Palace with three towers and the Palace multi–story Chaple of All Saints. The habilitation touched also the seat of Prague Bishops, whose residue has been discernable up to now in the front of the Old Provosts' Residence in the 3rd Courtyard.

After the siege of Prague Castle by Conrad of Znojmo (Konrád Znojemský) in 1142, during which fire broke out on the Castle "from a fire arrow", a reconstruction was made on St. George Basilica and Convent of Benedictines. The Abbess of the Convent used to be, after the example of its founder, the Prince's sister Mlada, a Princess of the Ruling House with a title of Princess–Abbess and with the right to crown the Queens of Bohemia; the Convent became a prestigious educational institution for girls of noble birth, and influenced significantly the development of Czech medieval culture, art and music.

T he ensuing 13th century brought an epoch of upsurge of the Czech Medieval State. Přemysl Otakar I succeeded in attaining the diplomatic recognition of the sovereignty of the Czech State, and of the succession to the Throne. His endeavors were crowned in 1212 by the issuing of a deed by Frederick II, called the Golden Bull of Sicily after the method of its sealing.

In the reign of Wenceslas I Prague Castle was a witness to the power struggle between the King and his son Přemysl Otakar.

The activity of the Přemyslids as founders during the economic upsurge concentrated upon the origination of new towns in the Land and upon construction of castles. Prague Castle was further enlarged westwards through the creation of a large settlement before the Castle, the Castle fortifications were improved, and to the original Romanesque Palace an aisle was added having arcades and nine, already Gothic pointed arches.

The Chapel of All Saints also was joined with the Palace.

After the fateful Battle in the Moravian Field, where Přemysl Otakar II lost his life, and after the ensuing disorganization in the Kingdom, it was finally the Přemysl Otakar's son Wenceslas II, who, again and firmly, concentrated the kingly power in his hands, and who, conducting a provident internal policy and eliminating, cleverly and in a step by step manner, his foreign enemies, brought the Land to a new prosperity. Wenceslas II was crowned King of Poland; he was offered the Hungarian Throne, which was finally succeeded to by his son Wenceslas III. Prague Castle then became the seat for a mighty ruler who aimed at the highest goals of the then Christian World. It only was the premature death of that King, never boasting of a good health, which disabled him from the succession to the Throne of the King of the Romans.

The architectural richness of Prague Castle and Prague and the rising power of the King of Bohemia were influenced to a large extent by silver which was then much exploited in several places in Bohemia, and first of all in Kutná Hora, which therefore became next the Town of Prague (Old Town) the richest and largest town in the Land. In 1300 the striking commenced of new coins of Czech silver, the so–called Prague Groschen, which became a choice specie.

After the death of Wenceslas II in 1305 his too young son Wenceslas III reigned for a short time, as he died of the hand of a hired assassin in 1306 in Olomouc, where the King's troops were gathering for a campaign in Poland.

After the short intervals of the reign of Rudolph of Austria and then Henry of Carinthia (Jindřich Korutanský) it was John of Luxemburg, son of Henry VII, Count of Luxemburg, King of the Romans and Holy Roman Emperor, who succeeded to the Czech Throne and took as her consort Elizabeth of the Přemyslids (Eliška Přemyslovna), the last unmarried Přemyslid Princess.

The very young John of Luxemburg came to Bohemia in 1310 with his troops, and after a short campaign against the followers supporting the ousted Henry of Carinthia he marched victoriously on December 6 in Prague, which got

The Vladislav Hall of the Royal Palace in Prague Castle – the paramount Late–Gothic work of Benedict Ried of Pístov, from the turn of the 15th and 16th centuries

in the meantime under control of his and Elizabeth's followers. As early as on February 7, 1311 John and Elizabeth were crowned by Peter of Aspelt, Archbishop of Mainz (Mayence), in St. Vitus Basilica in Prague Castle. The coronation feasts, however, had to take place in the Minorite Monastery of St. James down in Prague, as the Castle was basically uninhabitable after the fire of 1303 and after the recent castlekeeping by the Meissen troops who had been invited by the former King Henry of Carinthia to guard him.

The personage of John of Luxemburg can scarcely be characterized in short. He was renowned as the King diplomat, Warrior and Entrepreneur as well, and he represented the knightly virtues of that time and excelled in elegance, and the Christian World admired his courage, and deliberation in his behavior interchanged quite frequently with his impulsiveness. Though he cared, unless he needed further irretrievable advances from his subjects, of the management of domestic matters most time not much, he wore proudly the King of Bohemia's coat–of–arm insignia throughout all Royal Courts and theaters of war of Europe until August 26, 1346, when he, then already blind, moved on to the battle field, held between two horses of his courtiers as he had ordered, to lose his life with the sword in his hand, in the guards of French Chivalry in the Battle of Crécy against the English.

His son Charles was then already elected King of the Romans, and under King John's Last Will and Testament from 1340, and by the decision made by the Czech Assembly, and by homage acts by Prague and the Dukes of Silesia, he became also King of Bohemia. He already went through the thirteen years of reigning in Bohemia in place of his father, who almost always was not present, and he therefore had a great experience. When he was seven years old, his father carried him for upbringing away, to the French Royal Court where Queen Mary took care of him. Officially the upbringing purposes were indicated, however undertones involved were the fears of John of possible ousting him from the Throne in Bohemia and installing there his minor son.

The Charles' travel, however, was destined to bring the best consequences for Charles himself and for Bohemia's future as well. The perfect education, an extraordinary large overview for diplomacy, and cultural aspirations were what the future ruler of Bohemia did need. Roger des Rosiers, coming from Limoges, Abbot of Fécamp and later Pope Clement VI, who was "the talking head and educated man, decorated with his manners of many a nobility", became Charles' teacher. The Prince was favorably influenced by spiritual environment at the Sorbonne and also by the legal theory and practice of legists at the French Royal Court.

During the last two years before the return to Homeland, Father allowed him to taste the ruler's duties, at first in the County of Luxemburg, and later in the hot–weather environment of the Upper Italian Luxemburg Seigniory, where Charles deputized for his Father for some time. We mention the Charles' youth a little bit broader, in order that we could enlighten why the mere seventeen years old could revealed himself after his return to the Land as such a deliberate and vigorous ruler, the personage cultivated and thoughtful, the ruler who attained almost all what he had intended to.

Charles undertook decisive steps to clear the Royal Possessions of debts and gradually to redeem pledges. He commenced, in the fashion of the seat of French Kings, to revamp Prague Castle. At first he ordered to reconstruct entirely the Royal Palace. During this, Charles acted decisively as well as deliberately. He tried to join the new schemes and style elements with the stressing of tradition and genia loci, i. e. with the guarding of the distinctive local flavors.

The new Palace respected fully the older valuable portions of the construction, i. e. the Romanesque substructure and the preserved portions of the Palace of Přemysl Otakar II as well. The central room was the Great Hall, connected via a bridge to the neighboring Chapel of All Saints – mirabili opere, i. e. miracles are acting. The model for the refined construction with the rich batement lights paned with colorful vitrails was obviously the Saint–Chapelle in Paris.

Charles tried to strengthen comprehensively the rule of order and the international standing of the Land. An expression of his aspirations was the crowning of the hundreds of years old endeavors of the Přemyslid rulers to get out of the subordination to the Archbishopric

The balanced connection between the Romanesque and Baroque styles is demonstrated by the Baroque front and Romanesque towers of St. George's Basilica (bazilika sv. Jiří)
in Prague Castle

31

also legally – both by issuing the Rules of Crowning the Kings of Bohemia, and by the highest ecclesiastical authority, as Clement VI issued to that effect readily his Bull for his protégé.

Prague Castle, due to Charles, became the seat, the residential castle King of the Romans and, later, the Emperor of the Holy Roman Empire. Prague Castle lived in the bustle of diplomatic negotiations and kingly visits, in much same way as the newly built Emperor's Castle Karlštejn, near Prague and on the route to Nuremberg. The Charles' group of craftsmen (represented by the many–sided personage of Peter Parler (Petr Parléř), Master of St. Vitus Lodge, or by the painters Master Theodoric and Nicholas Wurmser of Strassbourgh, participated in the broad circle of numerous construction works in the Towns of Prague and throughout Bohemia and in other countries as well. Arts and crafts were upgrading extraordinarily, for instance the Prague goldsmiths' trade who took not only examples but also the impetuses of competitiveness from the works that had been imported from abroad. When Charles IV died in 1378, he left the deeds–delivering organism of his developing seat. However in the reign of his son Wenceslas IV the situation changed. The building and decorating activities continued, though at much slower paces, however the King himself moved in the Old Town to the King's Court (where the Community House stands now), which then became the Kingly Residence for the next one hundred years.

At the early stage of the Hussite Revolution (1419) the Castle housed a strong garrison of King Sigismund, who had not been recognized by the Hussites, and thus the Castle represented a lasting threat to the Hussite Prague. And therefore the Prague Hussites besieged the Castle in the spring of 1421, and as soon as the garrison in their hopeless situation surrendered, the Castle was occupied by the Hussites.

Large building modifications to Prague Castle, connected first of all with the name of Benedict Ried of Pístov, were being performed in the reign of the Kings of the Jagiello dynasty. As the first building work he undertook the reconstruction

of Mainz. As early as during his life Charles gained from Clement VI the issuing of the appropriate Bull. The educated Ernest of Pardubice (Arnošt z Pardubic), later the Chancellor and invaluable Counsellor to Charles, was appointed the first Metropolitan of Prague. In the same year, 1344, the foundation was laid of the new Cathedral of St. Vitus, whose construction was commenced by Matthias of Arras (Matyáš z Arrasu). Even there Charles advanced in an innovative way, as he respected the tradition of that place. In the new Cathedral under construction, preserved were fully the ring of chapels and the consecration of altars, first of all in St. Wenceslas Chapel, which became the spiritual center of the Land. Charles, by his personal experience during his stay at the French Royal Court, learnt how profound significance was attached to the royal coronation and the symbols of the coronation act.

The Crown of Czech Kings was consecrated to the Princely Patron, Charles IV had ordered to substantially remake the Crown with enriching with new precious stones and relics, and secured the statute and protection of the Crown of the Castle fortifications, as it was necessary to strengthen them with respect to the development in artillery. That related first of all to the strengthening of defense on both Gateways; an advanced fortification was built up at the West Gateway, and a barbacan was erected before the East Gateway. All the fortifications were completed with several artillery towers, from which the Daliborka Tower (used also as a jail) is the best known. However the Ried's mastership recorded itself immortally first of all during the reconstruction of the Royal Palace. The most important monuments from that time are the Vladislav Audience Parlor and the Vladislav Hall, the work from 1490 – 1502. Monumentally looks the vaults, and monumental in the same manner are the Riding Steps, i. e. the main ceremonial flight of stairs into the Vladislav Hall. The reconstruction of the west wing of the Royal Palace and the new Royal Oratory in the Cathedral of St. Vitus are obviously the works by Master Hans Spiess of Frankfort. Benedict Ried of Pístov then also built, between 1503 and 1510, the so–called Louis Wing of the Royal Palace. The Wing has already been built in a pure Renaissance style. The exterior of the building towards the City is divided by its Early Renaissance windows.

King Louis of Jagiello died tragically on his flight after the lost Battle of Hungarian Mohács against the Turks, and therefore Bohemia in 1526 was before the election of a new King. Ferdinand, Louis' brother– in–law, the Archduke of Austria and brother of the Emperor Charles V won the election. It is to be wondered that the representatives of the self–confident Estates State, non––Catholics by their decisive majority, proclaimed as King the determined Catholic and advocate of strong, centralized reign. Ferdinand signed the election declaration in which he obliged to respect both common law and written law; he was, however, decided to adhere to that promise as least as possible, in the interests of building the Central European Habsburg Monarchy. The attempts of recatholicizing, of restricting politically the Burgher Estates and the endeavors of centralization became the wrong side of Ferdinand's reign, which prolonged till the 1560s, when he already was, after his brother, the Empe-

ror of the Empire. In spite of that, the care about Prague Castle belongs to the prettier sides of his reign.

The antique medieval Castle changed into the Renaissance seat. Ferdinand commenced with building new Royal rooms west of the old Royal Palace, after the Stag Moat (Jelení příkop) he founded the Royal Garden with the Royal Summer Palace (Královský letohrádek), whose model was created by Paolo della Stella. The Royal Garden from the time after 1534 is the purest expression of the import of the Italian Renaissance north of the Alps; planted in the Garden are, after the example of Italian gardens, the Mediterranean flora and numerous exotics.

The implementation of that Renaissance project in Prague Castle was slowed down for a time by the fire which hit all the left–bank part of Prague on June 2, 1541. Ferdinand was in that time already fully engaged by his brother, the Emperor Charles V, in the matters in the Empire.

In August, 1547 Ferdinand, showing an unprecedented cruelty, dealt with the first revolt against the Habsburgs at the so–called Sanguinary Assembly of St. Bartholomew, and Prague Castle was a witness to those moments so humiliatory for Praguers. Ferdinand left in Prague his younger son, Ferdinand, the later Archduke of the Tirol, who together with his consort Philippa Welser kept their Renaissance Court, and who got close to the Czech environment and contributed to the development of Renaissance and humanistic thoughts in Prague Castle.

The process of building the Renaissance seat in Prague Castle continued after the fire also by the buildup of palaces of the high nobility, and continued also in the reign of the successor to Ferdinand, Maximilian II, and was crowned by Rudolph II. Prague Castle during the nearly thirty years of his reigning was again the Imperial Seat, trade revived, art and crafts were in blossom. The highly educated and cultivated Emperor, eroded with his serious and prolonged disease both physically and spiritually, was however retreating more and more into his privacy. The more was he so retreating, the more his taste applied in the erection of new buildings, decorations to buildings and gardens, and the more his passion for collecting the pieces of art grew. During the years of Rudolph II the Castle was ending the Renaissance chapter of its life, already on the soil of Mannerism.

Moreover to the reconstruction of the Chapel of All Saints and the decoration of the Cathedral of St. Vitus the Emperor ordered to build a new Palace with two large halls, the shorter Wing before the Church of St. Vitus with the Mathematical Tower and the adjacent, new Spanish Hall. Even the present Golden Lane (Zlatá ulička) originated. The Court of Rudolph II was one of the best–known centers of the European Mannerism, whose significance is only being appreciated at present. Prague became a crossroad for artists and craftsmen and scholars, alchemists and astrologers in particular, the marketplace of art dominated by the Emperor's passion.

The Emperor's need to collect the works of arts, products of nature, rarities and Antique finds was being satisfied through tens of agents.

The Emperor was a generous patron, Maecenas, and so lived he surrounded with not only scholars and craftsmen, but also charlatans and swindlers. In Prague then settled the large colony of Italian artists, craftsmen, carvers, stone masons, constructors and stuccoworkers, and a lot of others came from Rhineland or the Netherlands, and a number of them began to feel at home in Bohemia for ever.

Beyond the Castle Walls, however, conflicts were notifying pertinaciously of their existence – the wars against the Turks, and first of all, the European Religious Crisis, which tossed even the Kingdom of Bohemia. The majority of the non–Catholic Estates stood against the smaller but influential count of the Catholic nobility, the so–called Spanish Side. It is true that the Reformed succeeded in exacting the Imperial Charter on Religious Liberty from Rudolph, however a short time later, the Emperor, then already contrite with his disease and powerless, yielded in mutual rivalry to his brother Matthias, and he short died, in 1612. In 1614 in the Castle built is the huge Matthias Gateway (Matyášova brána),

with which at that same time a new architectural style, the Baroque, notifies Prague of itself.

The conflict between the Habsburg House and the Czech Estates opposition, all but exceptions Protestants, reached its climax on May 23, 1618 with the Defenestration, i. e. throwing of Royal Governors, Catholics Jaroslav Bořita of Martinice and William Slavata of Chlum, out of the second––story windows of Louis Wing in the Royal Palace into the Castle Moat.

The victorious Estates then called on Frederick V of the Palatinate, the then leader of the German Union of Protestants to the Throne of Bohemia, and he arrived in Prague on October 31, 1619. The new ruler with his consort Elizabeth, daughter of James I, King of England, was crowned King of Bohemia at the Cathedral of St. Vitus. However his reign on Prague Castle lasted for a short time only, over one winter – and after this he was called the Winter King. The defeat at the White Mountain on November 8, 1621 ended the Rising of Czech Estates, and who did not save himself by flight or timely conversion or through mighty Catholic intercessors, was awaited by the Executioner on June 21, 1621 on the Old Town Square, or in a better case, by the forced exodus from Bohemia, without any means. The Land was enthralled by administrative and military oppression, and forced recatholicization went on.

he victorious Habsburgs degraded the Kingdom of Bohemia into a mere nonself–governing province. The Thirty Years' War depopulated and plundered the Land. The troops of Königsmark, the Swedish General, succeeded to loot Rudolph's Collections and other treasures in the Castle and the Lesser Town during the winter (1648) before the Peace Treaty of Westphalia.

In spite of that situation and already before the end of the Thirty Years' War, on the Castle began the construction of a new Palace (for Mary Anne of Spain) from the plans by G. Mattei. In 1680 the Convent Church of St. George got its Baroque gable facade on the frontage, with the sculpture of the saint, and the Chapteral Provostship also obtained its Baroque appearance. During the 1720s the Chapel of St. John Nepomuk was added to the Baroque St. Georges frontage. Lobkowicz Palace also was reconstructed in Baroque style in 1670s, and at the end of the 17th century the Castle and Gardens on the north side were encircled with a continuous strip of bastion fortifications. The construction of St. Vitus' Cathedral met with its revival, as the Emperor Leopold I, having obeyed a prophecy of "who would complete the Cathedral, would oust the Turks from Europe", laid the base stone for completing the Cathedral.

Moreover to the constructions of palaces and ecclesiastical buildings, during the Baroque period also several smaller Chapels originated in the Castle, and the exteriors and interiors had shone with numerous new Baroque sculptures.

Later the Castle was much damaged during the Wars of Austrian Succession and the Seven Years' War, when it was bombarded by the enemy troops. In particular during the siege of Prague in 1744 and then in 1757 the fire of Prussian artillery caused serious damages.

In spite of this already in 1753 in the reign of Empress Maria Theresa the magnificent reconstruction of the Castle was commenced under a Viennese constructor, N. F. Paccassi. The Castle panorama obtained its mighty almost classicizing appearance. The period of Baroque therefore ended on the Castle with the monumental art reconstruction.

owever it was only in the 19th century, when finally the permanently postponed intention of completing the Cathedral of St. Vitus was successfully implemented. Under the influence of a patriotic Canon, Pešina of Čechorod, the Association for Completing St. Vitus Cathedral was founded, and on October 1, 1873 the base stone was laid for construction, which lasted till 1929. Through the Paccassi's extensive reconstruction of the Castle and the completion of the Cathedral, Prague Castle obtained the appearance of the present–day panorama.

Prague Castle, after the origination of independent Czechoslovakia in 1918, became the seat of the President of the Republic. The Castle is the most important monument in Prague, the place which symbolizes the government, cultural and historical tradition as well as the present freedom times.

The frontage of the Palace of the Archbishop on Hradčany
Square excels in its fine Rococo facade.

HRADČANY

Since in the time of the Battle done before Prague Castle
in the reign of Henry of Carinthia an open was still there,
it is to find the beginning of Hradčany and the Town
in the times of King John. And Hradčany, however, was not
a Royal Town from the very beginning; instead, Hradčany
was a subject little town belonging to the Burgravate
of Prague. For that reason it appears to me as the most likely
that the little town was founded by a Burgrave of Prague
for increasing the profits from the possessions pertaining
to the Authority, and it appears undoubtedly the founder
was Hynek Berka of Dubá, who hold that post
for the longest time in the reign of John, and who at that
same time was also the Administrator of the Land.

FROM THE HISTORY OF THE CITY OF PRAGUE
BY WENCESLAS VLADIVOJ TOMEK

One of the oldest settlements in the area
of Prague began to grow probably
on the land west of Prague Castle.
In that places the terrain is rising
slightly from the Castle's site, and it
widens to the free space naturally demarcated
both south and north by the natural slopes. The
original before–Castle settlement on the slope
of Hradčany may have existed as early as
in the 11th century; however, a convincing
evidence is missing. In any case sometime after
1320 the Burgrave of Prague, Hynek Berka
of Dubá, founded Hradčany as a subject town,
partially walled in, and with three Gates through
which the routes entered the town. Craftsmen,
servants of the Castle, clergymen and also
noblemen, all those whose duties at the Royal
Court or at St. Vitus Cathedral commanded them
to be any time near, began to move in the town.
In the Town of Hradčany's Book mentioned is already for 1353 the Parochial Church of St. Bene-

37

dict, which stood on the southwest corner of the present–day square Hradčanské náměstí.

After the Charles' splendid Fortifications had been built up which encompassed the left bank part of Prague west of the original Strahovská Gateway (at Hradčany), between the Fortifications of the Convent of Strahov and the Charles' new Wall, grew a suburb called Pohořelec, and the new Walls covered also the area laying northwest of Hradčany, when later, in the reign of Rudolph II, a new Hradčany's quarter originated – the picturesque Nový Svět (New World).

The actual disaster for the little town of Hradčany was the beginning of the Hussite Revolution (1419–1420), as during the time of battles for the supremacy over Prague Castle, Hradčany was burnt out and half demolished mostly by the Hussites, partly by the Royal Garrison.

After that, Hradčany recovered at a very slow pace from the disaster. And it was as late as in the reign of the Jagiello and in connection with the building activities in the Castle, when that little town revived. Then also the Town Hall was built up in the higher part of Hradčanské Square (Hradčanské náměstí). Pohořelec, however, stayed abandoned.

The upsurge of the little town was however slowed down by the great fire which got hold of Lesser Town and from there skipped over to Prague Castle and Hradčany, in 1541. A large number of the newly erected or inhabited houses became a mere ash. And it was no earlier than in the second half of the 16th century when a new rise began of the little town, which was crowned in 1598 when the town was raised to the Royal Town.

The burghers, naturally, built for themselves a new Town Hall, that time already in the Renaissance style, and namely to the right, where Loretánská Street joins Hradčanské Square. In that time splendid Renaissance noblemen's Palaces grew, for instance Lobkowicz Palace (later, Schwarzenberg Palace) or Grysperks Palace, later bought for the restored Prague Archbishopric by Ferdinand I, or the House of Christopher Popel of Lobkowicz (later, Sternberg Palace).

The Renaissance gables, sgraffitti and rustications of Schwarzenberg Palace on Hradčany Square (Hradčanské náměstí) – from the second half of the 16th century, Architect Agostino Galli

During the Thirty Years' War and also during further campaigns the Town of Hradčany never remained saved from the devastating behavior of the troops. And in spite of that, Hradčany nowadays is a telling proof of the beautifulness of the Prague Renaissance, Baroque and newer architectural styles.

The north side of Hradčany Square is dominated by the Palace of Archbishop, built since 1562, when the Archbishopric of Prague was administered again, by Anthony Archbishop Brus of Mohelnice. The Palace had undergone a further significant structural modification in the time of John Frederick of Wallenstein, when the Palace was given the Early Baroque appearance by Architect John Baptist Mathey. Nowadays the Palace can boast of the Late Baroque apperance by Architect J. J. Wirch from 1764 – 1765 (at the expense of Anthony Archbishop Příchovský).

Through the passage in the left side rizalit of the Palace of Archbishop we can get to Sternberg Palace, the important Baroque structure built for Wenceslas Adalbert of Sternberg by Architects G. B. Allipradi and G. Santini.

The National Gallery with its collections of old European art is located in the Palace. The upsurge and completeness are excellent in particular in the collections of: Italian Primitivists, old Dutch Masters, Italian cinquecento, Flemish and Dutch painting of the 17th century, and behind–the–Alps Renaissance painting. A separate section represents French painting of the 19th and 20th centuries.

n the north side of the Quarter stand a row of Baroque houses of canons of St. Vitus Chapter up to the late Renaissance Palace of Counts of Martinic, which stands at the elbow to Kanovnická Street and was adapted around the mid–17th century by the then lady owner, Helen Barbara Kostomlatská of Vřesovice. Down the Street Kanovnická the visitor can get to the Baroque Church of St. John Nepomuk, which is the splendid temple structure by Gillean Ignatius Dienzenhofer (Kilián Ignác Dienzenhofer) from 1720– 1729, and further to the buildings of the nearby Convent of the Ursuline Nuns. The magnificent fresco which decorates

the interior of the Cathedral is a work by Wenceslas Lawrence Reiner (Václav Vavřinec Reiner) from 1727–1728.

The whole west side of Hradčanské Square is formed by the frontage of the Palace of Dukes of Tuscany, and it is the main frontage of the Palace which dominates the whole place.

The south side front is occupied by two Palaces of Schwarzenberg, from which the larger, with the decorated, picturesque gables, with sgraffiti and rustications,dates from the second half of the 16th century, as a work by Constructor Agostino Galli. It is one of the best examples of the domestication of Italian Renaissance architecture in Bohemia. The other Palace on the rim of the Square opposite to the Castle is a Classicistic structure from the beginning of the 19th century, which was built at the expense of William Florentin Archbishop Salm––Salm.

Behind the complex of the former Convent of the Carmelite Nuns in the southwest corner of the Square join two communications – the first communication, for pedestrians, the broad steps, called Town Hall Steps, lead through picturesque elbows and passages to Lesser Town, the other communication, Loretánská Street, is the main way in Hradčany now. On their intersection point stands the Renaissance building of the former Town Hall of Hradčany. The streets mostly lined with Renaissance palaces and houses, come to Loretto Square (Loretánské náměstí), called after Loretto, the pilgrimage place. The work in the style of the Roman Baroque in the 17th century was built from the plans of Architect J. B. Mathey by Constructor G. A. Canevalle at the expense of Michael Count Oswald Thun in the 17th and 18th centuries. Arcades circumvent the small House, originally at grade, and later multi–story with seven Chapels. The nucleus is a copy of Bramante's Casa Santa, the pilgrimage Holy House in Italian Loretto. The Prague Casa Santa was built during 1626 – 1627 by Constructor G. B. Orsi at the expense of Benigna, Countess of Lobkowicz. By enlarging the main Chapel on the centerline of the building with the participation of Christopher Dienzenhofer in the twenties of the 18th century the Church of the Nativity, in whose enlargements and modifications already took part Gillean Ignatius Dienzenhofer. On the Tower of Loretto sound the famous Chimes each hour the melody of Marian Litany, which is inseparable from the atmosphere of Hradčany. The Loretto houses also a large collection of chasubles and liturgical vessels from the time of the Renaissance and Baroque. A symbol of the place as well as the collection of the Loretto Treasury is the famous Diamond Monstrance, called also the Prague Sun. The Monstrance was designed by a Viennese Architect, Johann Bernard Fischer von Erlach, and is covered with six and a half thousand diamonds. The oldest goldsmith's masterpiece is the Late Gothic calix with enamel figures of the Czech Patrons from the beginning of the 16th century.

ith the Baroque splendor of the Loretto contrasts the spectacular simplicity of the nearby Convent of the Capuchins from the time after 1600, established on the land of Margaret of Lobkowicz. In the gable wall of the Convent's little Church of the Angelic Virgin Mary walled in are, to the memory, the cannon balls which remind of bombarding Prague by the Prussian Troops of Frederick the Great in the Wars with Maria Theresa of the Austrian Succession. At present the little Church has perfectly harmonious interior and during Christmas it is for its famous "Bethlehem" visited by a number or people.

The whole north part of Loretto Square is taken by the monumental, plastically conceived frontage of Černín Palace, which for Humprecht John Duke Černín, Emperor's Ambassador to Venice, was planned and built by F. Caratti with the participation of John Decapauli and Abraham Leuther in 1669–1677.

The Founder's descendants continued with the modifications and decorations to the Palace till the 18th century. In 1742 and 1757 the Palace was heavily damaged at first by the French Army and later by the Prussian bombardment. In 1851 the Palace was sold to Treasury and converted to the barracks. The abandoned Palace was taken in 1928 into the care of the Czechoslovakian State, and in 1934 the complex, restored in a reverent way, was given to the Ministry of Foreign Affairs.

North of the Palace lies the charming suburb of Hradčany, composed of picturesque houses of Baroque appearance and smaller Palaces, Nový Svět, and west of the Palace there is the triangular square Pohořelec mentioned already earlier. First of all the south side of the Square, which is with its houses adjacent to the building of the former Strahov Brewery, and which continues up to the Baroque entrance Gateway in the complex of Strahov Monastery, is ornamented with the Statue of St. Norbert. The nearby beautiful Gothic–Renaissance Church of St. Rochus (kostel sv. Rocha), built from the scheme prepared by G. M. Filippi, dates from the Rudolph's times.

Strahov Monastery was founded in 1140, from the initiative of Henry Zdík, Bishop of Olomouc, by King Vladislav who placed there the Convent of the then new Premonstratensian Order. The founding by the King is indicated both by the strategical importance of that place (Strahov designates "Watchmen's Post" – or the hill which controls access to Prague from the west) and by the extraordinary scope and architectural richness of the walled–in complex. Strahov Monastery ranked among the richest Monasteries in Bohemia, was renowned as a center of scholarship, and was the center of the Province of the Order. The Monastery's nucleus is the Abbey's Cathedral of the Assumption, originally the Romanesque Basilica from the 12th century, rebuilt during the Gothic, Renaissance and Baroque times into the present–day appearance.

he rarest valuableness kept in Strahov Monastery is its Library with a number of very old manuscripts (for instance, the oldest parchment Evangeliary from the 9th century), incunabula and later prints, to an extraordinary extent in both the ecclesiastical region and natural and social sciences. The Library's funds are placed mostly in the historical interiors with original decorations and movables. After the tens of years the Premonstratensians are returning between the walls of the Monastery. A beautiful view of Prague opens from Strahov Monastery. On the rim of the view on the left is the dominant of Prague Castle, on the right there are the green slopes of the hill Petřín.

One of the views of Prague Castle: the Cathedral of St. Vitus
(svatovítská katedrála) protrudes high above the Palaces
in Hradčany and in the Castle

Strahov Monastery (Strahovský klášter) with the Church
of the Assumption (kostel Nanebevzetí Panny Marie) show
Baroque appearances now; however, the Romanesque
nucleus is from the beginning of the 12th century. The view
from Prague Castle indicates the largeness of the Strahov
Monastery complex

The Castle complex is entered from Hradčany Square
(Hradčanské náměstí) through the Matthias Gateway
(Matyášova brána) built at the beginning of the 17th century.
On the left is the Palace of the Archbishop, a notable Late
Baroque structure

The bronze equestrian statue of St. George in the courtyard
of Prague Castle is a copy of a Gothic original work.
The brothers George and Martin of Klausenberg made
the copy during the seventies of the 14th century

The vestibule entrance of the Golden Gate (Zlatá brána),
by Peter Parler (Petr Parléř) from the years 1368 to 1370

45

The heart of the Cathedral of St. Vitus is the Chapel
of St Wenceslas (svatováclavská kaple); in the interior
of the Chapel stands the statue of St Wenceslas

The Gothic statue of St. Wenceslas in the Chapel
of St. Wenceslas is a work by Henry Parler
(Jindřich Parléř) from 1373

47

The Cathedral of St. Vitus: view through the presbytery
of the vaulting, works by Matthias of Arras
(Matyáš z Arrasu) and Peter Parler

The Hall of Columns in the Royal Palace in Prague Castle,
from the time around 1390

Over the Chaples which form the close to the Cathedral
of St. Vitus grows a forest of finial pinnacles and buttresses
of the buttress system

The Renaissance Royal Summer Palace and the Royal Garden originated during the reign of Ferdinand I. The Summer Palace is the loveliest and oldest Renaissance structure north of the Alps

The huge mass of St. Vitus Cathedral protrudes above the roofs of Hradčany

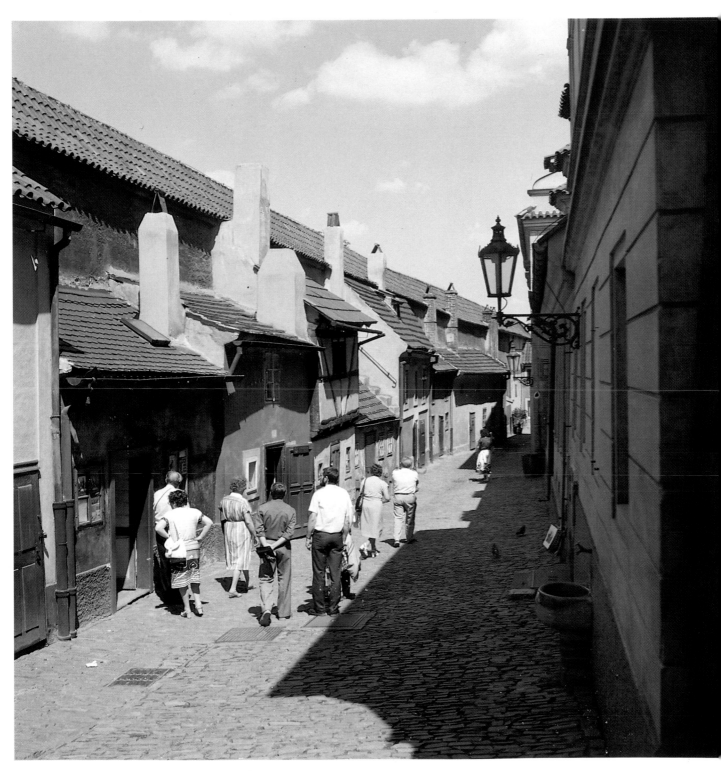

Golden Lane, with its bizzare little houses (from the 16th century) of the Castle Soldiers or alchemists, is the most frequently visited place in Prague Castle

The Black Tower (Černá věž) dates from as early as
the Romanesque fortifications of Prague Castle. During
the reign of Charles IV the Tower was called "Golden",
because its roof was covered with nailed gilt lead– sheets

Úvoz, the little street in Hradčany, originated from
the ancient trail leading from one ford on the Vltava
River upwards and then westwards below Prague
Castle. The street is lined with petty palaces and burgher
houses showing various architectural styles

55

The characteristic panorama of Prague reminds of the time
of Charles IV: the Cathedral of St. Vitus and the Stone Bridge
called, in the 19th century, Charles Bridge after
the great Ruler

THE OLD TOWN OF PRAGUE

King Wenceslas in the first year and for more years of his
reign loved very much the clergy, both secular and
of orders, and with more pleasure he venerated God's
churches and their servants. However in the course of time,
when his father had already taken the way of dead body,
he ordered to wall in the Town of Prague, and to fortify
in stone or wood the other market villages, which are called
towns in our common language. In his reign the good peace
governed for many years.

FROM THE SECOND CONTINUATION
IN THE CHRONICLE OF COSMAS

The beginnings of dense settlement along the right bank of the Vltava can be assumed as early as in the late 10th century. The centerlines of that settlement were the trails leading to fords on the Vltava and probably also to the first predecessor of the present–day Charles Bridge – the wooden bridge, over which already then the body of the assassinated Prince Wenceslas was supposedly carried to Prague Castle. A record of Chronicler Cosmas from 1091 on two trader settlements in the area below Prague Castle indicates that in the first case it was probably a settlement in the foreground nearest to the Castle and that in the other case the settlement was meant on the connecting line between Vyšehrad and a ford on the Vltava somewhere between the now existing Mánes Bridge and Charles Bridge, where the route led further to Prague Castle. This should also correspond to the growing importance of that right–bank area after the temporary transfer of the Princely Seat to Vyšehrad in the reign of Prince Wratislaw II. At that same time a settlement already existed of German traders on the Riverside, and probably more settlements existed there, as indicated in the Cosmas' narrative on the famous arrival of Břetislav II to Prague in 1092, mentioning the "dancing crowds, deployed over various crossroads or at the churches below the Castles".

At the end of the 11th century the marketplace

A Gothic covered walk in the oldest part of the Old Town, in the so–called Gall quarter mentioned by the Chronicler was, probably and roughly, located in the place of the present–day Old Town Square, and still after 1100 it was the place where moreover to the Saturday markets also public rallies were held, and where in cases of need the troops were being gathered. For instance, in 1105 on "the large marketplace between Praha (the Castle) and Vyšehrad" camping were the troops of Svatopluk Přemyslid.

However after 1100 the area below the Castle enters a new developmental stage, which is bound by the year 1230, when the construction of Walls commenced. The main trait of that Romanesque Prague is the concentration of settlement in the area of marketplace and between the present–day crossroad Perštýn and the bridge, which was replaced by the stone Judith Bridge around 1170.

round the mid–12th century the buildup started of that concentration of settlement, and at the beginning of the 13th century the Old Town settlement, then called Prague Below Castle or Mezihradí ("Between Castles"), was the best distinguished body of settlement in the entire area of Prague. The keen economic activities and the buildup of wealthiness of some inhabitants stimulated building activities and influenced the population increase, which relied upon the large immigration and represented an accompanying trait of prosperity.

The existence of permanent stopping–places of foreign traders, allowed by the Princely Privileges, strengthened the importance of the marketplace. The foreign traders used to take refuge in the large Princely Court called Týn, which was mentioned for the first time in the reign of Prince Bořivoj II. The import and transit duty, the so–called ungeld, was collected there, and from this followed the name of Ungelt for the Court. The Court served to accommodate traders and to enable them their rest after the tiresome travels, and this brought the Court also the Latin sobriquet curia laeta, "the Midway Court", or also hospitum.

The architectural richness of a large portion of the below–Castle area on the right bank of the Vltava, the concentration of population around the main marketplace, the buildup of street communication network and further elements has decided the urban trait of settlement since the mid–12th century. Though in that Romanesque Prague shown were the large urban building development and the strong population, and both trades and crafts developed, the generally binding legal standards which could influence the collective life of the entire below–Castle area had not yet asserted themselves. It was however just that trait which was telling the medieval towns from the lower–type settlements.

The construction of Walls, which was commenced by King Wenceslas I after 1230, was the key event in the process of transformation of the below–Castle area into the Town of Prague, civitas Pragensis, as it was called at first after the Castle. The Walls however did not have a mere military significance; they meant the further strengthening of external and internal unity of the municipal area, and thus the significant legal and social prerequisites for the collective development of urban life were being created.

The Wall strip around the Town was 1700 meters long and encircled an area of some 140 hectares. The double wall was strengthened by the multitude of towers, some of which were rising as high as thirty meters, and the entry into the Town was guarded by two Gates. Approximately at that same time during the process of completing settlement the mostly German colonists founded the Settlement at St. Gall, which retained for some time even its self–government independence. The Walls were completed by 1241, and that completed the external transformation of the below–Castle area. Irrespective of the military function the fortified Town became a seat entity quite different than the earlier scattered partial settlements. Inside the Town, trade and crafts developed keen, Convents were growing and next to the main marketplace the auxiliary marketplaces were appearing.

The advent of the Gothic style in Prague and Bohemia is symbolized by the founder's deed of King Wenceslas I: in 1233 he provided the Order of St. Clare of Assissi's Nuns, who were introduced in Bohemia by St. Agnes of Bohemia, his sister and first Abbess, with a large area for erecting their Convent. The Convent, though originally intended for the Clare Nuns, was later partially occupied also with the Minorites. Agnes' activities were reflected both in the half-century of erecting the Convent and also in the spiritual, cultural and political life of the Land. The educated Princess, who resigned the proposals for advantageous dynastical marriages and decided to give preference to serve Christ and the poor and sick, was a personage of the 13th century by her overview, contacts and diplomatic art.

In the reign of Přemysl Otakar II a large upsurge of Prague occurred. The Towns of Prague, by a witness of a contemporary Chronicler, "managed in his reign to become very rich and affluent, which was contributed to by the noise of the Court well stocked and by the largeness of the Otakar's Empire… giving even the foreigners from the very distant parts the cause for visiting the Capital of Bohemia". Trade and the weekday markets were controlled by domestic traders, and under the pressure from the craftsmen, who formed the numerous layer of inhabitants at the end of the 13th century, the development started of municipal trades system, whose pillars became the Guilds.

Extraordinarily large building activities dominated the Town in particular from the mid–13th century. In that time the new construction of the Convent and Church of St. James originated and the reconstruction of the Church of Our Lady Before Týn was commenced, and keen building activities ruled in the entire complex of St. Agnes Convent. Then the Order of Dominicans founded the Church of St. Clement near Judith Bridge, and nearby established their Convent also the Knights of the Cross With the Red Star.

The upsurge of trade and manufacture in the reign of Přemysl Otakar II (1253–1278) created favorable conditions for the increase in the property and finance capabilities of some burghers. The rapid property and social rise of burgher patricians, profiting also from their share in the extraction of silver and in the transactions with precious metals, led to the upsurge

in the burgher land coverage. Even there the Gothic introduced gradually its forms, layouts and dimensions, though not as easy as in the constructions of sacral types.

The process of internal unification to the legal effect reached its full maturity around 1287. Then already at the head of Town stood the Royal Magistrate, and as usual with twelve Aldermen appointed by the King he administered justice and the municipal government. It is not uninteresting that in that year King Wenceslas II imposed his ban on carrying weapons, which however was soon not adhered to. Nuremberg Law was considered as the legal basis for unification, in reality it was however the so–called "Swabian Mirror", which underwent local changes and made concessions also to the effect of Magdeburg Law. However even after that unification the municipal area did not become a fully unified entity, as small islands remined inside within the jurisdiction of the Church Authorities.

In spite of the increasing wealthiness the burghers did not succeed in weakening the role of the Royal Magistrate and strengthening the influence of the Aldermen's Council. Nor did Wenceslas II yield, having been asked in 1296 to allow the establishment of aldermen's Town Hall, though basically he rather showed his favor to the Towns and supported, more or less, their development. However the King's unwillingness stemmed from his disbelief in political liberties of cities. The growing wealthiness of the patricians at the beginning of 14th century elevated gradually their political ambitions which were exceeding municipal dimensions.

After the death of Wenceslas III in 1306 and therefore dying out of the Přemyslids on the spear side even the Prague patriciate divided into two rival groups, from whom that one headed by the Velflovic House supported Henry of Carinthia as candidate for the Czech Throne while the Olbramovic House and others sided with the candidacy of the Habsburgs. The result of the fierce fight over getting power and influence upon the new ruler of Bohemia was that the Town did not experience the peace needed for economic life and actual fights occurred

Present–day appearance of the Great Hall in the Carolinum.
The Hall was built around 1383

several times. The fights over Prague from the beginning of the 14th century however also showed that the fortification system was as successful that it was possible to get the Town under control only with help by allies inside the Walls.

The victory of John of Luxemburg in that battle of the Bohemian Crown brought the Town the desired peace, however soon afterwards it showed the knightly King would ask permanently for money which should be delivered as donations or nonrealistic loans. The Prague Burghers had bestowed costly jewelry totaling 120 talents of silver on the Royal married Couple already during coronation, that was however the mere beginning. On the other hand the broadminded Luxemburg returned Praguers' favors by granting new privileges, untile and finally, on September 18, 1338 and in the distant Amiens, he issued his Royal Permit for the Old Town burghers allowing them to establish their own Town Hall. That was the crowning of the previous self––governmental endeavor shown by the Old Town, and when in 1341 he gave his consent to the preparation of a new, own Legal Code, and granted the Old Town burghers judicial sovereignty over other towns, that meant the recognition of exceptional position of the Old Town in the Kingdom. And therefore the burghers bought, from Volflin of Stone and without any delay, the corner house on the marketplace, and established their Town Hall in that house.

n 1346 Charles IV son of John of Luxemburg, was elected King of the Roman, and short afterwards and still in that same year, after the death of his father in the Battle of Crécy, he was also elected King of Bohemia. Prague became, all of a sudden, an actual residential City and that was only confirmed by Charles' building activities.

Also the Old Town was not bypassed by the magnificent founder's deeds of Charles IV. So first of all in 1348 Charles founded there the University, in order that – how the Deed of University's Foundation read – "the inhabitants of the Kingdom of Bohemia should not be forced to beg alms in foreign countries, and could, instead, find in the Kingdom a table set to entertain them". Already during the life of its founder the University, the first one of that kind north of the Alps, started to attract novice scholars from the Lands of the Czech Crown and also from neighboring or even the more distant parts of the then Christian World, and became a center of spiritual ferment.

Prague Charles University then became, at the beginning of the 14th century, the center of learned opposition responding to the crisis phenomena in society and simultaneously activating and unifying the malcontents from the various layers of Prague population and the entire Kingdom. The attitudes of Czech Masters (professors) in many respects started from the views of John Wyclif, an English reformer whose writings were brought to Bohemia to a larger extent by Jerome of Prague (Jeroným Pražský).

The official administration seat of Charles University (Karlova univerzita) has until now been the Carolinum, whose nucleus is the oldest building of Charles College from the second half of the 14th century, the Gothic house of Johlin Rothlev, master of the mint. That time of the beginnings is reminded of by the Grand Hall with the oriel shrine on the ground floor. In the courtyard of the Carolinum there is now the Statue of Master John Hus by Sculptor Karel Lidický.

In 1357 Charles IV commenced the construction of a new stone bridge over the Vltava. That bridge was to be substituted for Judith Bridge, destroyed by floods, and was to connect the Towns of Prague on the right bank of the Vltava with the Lesser Town of Prague or Little Quarter, as that town was called from 1348, when Charles founded the New Town beyond the Walls of the Greater Town of Prague or the Old Town and on the strip of land between Vyšehrad and On the Riverside, the Vltava's bank. Proven again during the construction of the bridge and its monumental Bridge Tower on the Old Town end was the mastership of Peter Parler and his building Lodge. Charles IV charged the Old Town Burghers with the care about the bridge and its defense, and on the left bank of the river he incorporated the relatively large bridgehead including Kampa (or Ostrov, as the island was then also called) among the areas administered by the Old Town.

After the foundation of the New Town, the Old Town remained the settlement with the supremacy of the patriciate and the better–to––do burgher families: the Old Town was the bulwark of trade, and therefore Charles IV, in order that he could stress the importance of the Old Town, decided to increase for the Old Town burghers the number of Aldermen from twelve to eighteen. Keen building activities ruled in the Old Town, the Town Hall Tower with its oriel shrine was erected, in the burghers land coverage the wealthiness of burghers manifested itself in the new houses of the mainly hall type with large common dining–parlors. The King's Court was also erected in the Old Town. Almost all of the Old Town churches were being reconstructed and the Gothicizing showed in the large project for the Church of Our Lady Before Týn and also in the reconstructions of the Convent and Church of Saints James (kostel sv. Jakuba), Gall (sv. Havla) and Giles (sv. Jiljí) and other Old Town churches. Charles' ideas of its residential seat were gradually coming true. The urban population also grew, and the Prague conurbation, dominated by the Old Town, was profiting from the economic prosperity of Charles' reign.

However the population density of the city brought along also the danger of insufficient substenance for a large portion of the urban wage––earning labor who came, to win jobs, at the beginning of the great prosperity. Also the discrepancies grew between the patriciate and the craftsmen, who tried to exercise their economic upsurge for a greater share of influence upon administering the Town. The internal inconstistencies were strengthening during the reign of Charles' son Wenceslas IV, mainly after 1400, when Prague ceased to be the residential city of King of the Romans and Holy Roman Emperor and when the upsurge of the reign of the Great Emperor was in the realms beyond recall. Many a construction commenced in the reign of Charles remained uncompleted: sales opportunities were lowering for craftsmen and traders, job opportunities for the poorer layers of urban population were decreasing. The retreat of Prague from the political sunlight showed the dependence of its economy upon local consumption, whose decline afflicted all layers of Prague's population. The cheerless situation sharpened the internal inconsistencies in that population.

And yet the Old Town's economic position had strong foundations and due to this the Old Town did not feel the economic stagnation as hard as the New Town, in whose population prevalent were craftsmen and the poorer wage

The Ecce homo sculpture (from the period after 1400)
is located in the Old Town Hall

earning labor layers. And therefore it was not by chance that later the Hussite Revolution was announced with the revolutionary outburst just in the New Town, as the contemplations about how to make remedies for the matters were there nearer to actions. During the Revolution also the New Town always was the more radical in their calls than the Old Town of Prague.

After 1434, when the Old Town was in the ranks of victors of Lipany while the New Town was among those defeated, the Old Town Government had a not negligible share in the succession of Sigismund of Luxemburg (Zikmund Lucemburský) to the Czech Throne, and Sigismund returned that by restoring the old and granting new privileges. In the kingless period, which occurred after the death of Sigismund's son–in–law and successor to the Czech Throne, Albert of Austria (Albrecht Rakouský), the role of the Old Town as the center of the Kingdom had grown immensely. The politics and power upsurge of the Old Town burghers was also confirmed by the reality that it was the Old Town Hall where in 1458 the King of Bohemia was elected from the rank of Czech Calixtin – George of Poděbrady.

The privileged position at the head of the Town Burgher's Estates in the Kingdom was watched over by the Old Town even int he reign of the Jagiello House, and it was necessary to fight within the Estates State fiercely with the aristocrats for that position. The Jagiello period also meant the further unusual upsurge of building activities in the Town. The important political role of burghers in the post–Hussite Estates State and their wealthiness were matched with the high cultural level of the burghers' environment. The Late Gothic in the works of Masters Benedict Ried of Pístov or Matthias Rejsek left its traces for ever in the Town. Dominant in particular are the Late Gothic finish, reconstruction and enlargement of the Old Town Hall, the restoration of the Clock by Master John (Hanuš) around 1490, or the construction of the so–called New Tower at the Old Town Royal Court (the present––day Powder Tower – Prašná brána), commenced in 1475 under the supervision of Prague Constructor Wenceslas and completed by Master Matthias Rejsek. Architectural activities revived in the Convent of the Knights of the Cross With the Red Star near Charles Bridge. Also the Bethlehem Chapel (Betlémská kaple), a remembrance of Master John Hus, was modified in the Late Gothic style. The building activities also ran in burgher houses, and the architectural modifications concentrated first of all in the central area of the Old Town, mainly in the seats of Old Town Patricians.

After the succession of the Habsburgs to the Czech Throne the new Ruler Ferdinand I started to impose, systematically, bounds upon the political position of the Town. In 1534 he ceased the temporary connection of the Old and New Towns under a single Aldermen's Administration. Ferdinand's policy against the Town provoked discontentedness and Praguers were getting more and more into opposition to the Ruler. The variance got its peak in 1547, when the revolt of the Old Town, other Royal Towns and the majority of Czech Noblemen showed inter alia in the refusal, by Prague and its aristocratic allies, to give, by their troops, support to Ferdinand, who was ally to his brother, Emperor Charles V in the war with the so–called Association of Schmalkalden. However, all the revolt ended with a disaster never met before in the history of the Town.

Sixt of Ottersdorf, Old Town Chancellor who later became Chronicler of those events, was even threatened with execution, and moreover, a number of burghers were imprisoned, some were banished from the country, possessions of others were confiscated. The Municipal Governments in the Royal Towns were subordinated to the Authority of King's Magistrates, and in the old and New Towns also to King's Administrators. The position of Prague, having been built over long years, collapsed overnight. The political glory of the Town and its important role in the Community of the Estates ended.

In the second half of the 16th century and in the early 17th century the Old Town had still retained its Gothic traits. However the Renaissance architecture penetrated gradually also the Old Town. The well–to–do burghers had enough means to match the noblemen in the architectural richness of burgher houses and the habitation style as well. For instance, this is witnessed by: the lovely, decorated with sgraffiti

House at the Minute (dům U minuty), standing next to the Aldermen's Buildings; the House at the Two Golden Bears (dům U dvou zlatých medvědů) with its splendid portal; the House at the French Crown in Charles Lane (Karlova ulice), where Astronomer John Kepler lived; the Týn College (Týnská škola) on the Old Town Square; or the Granovský House (dům Granovských) behind the Týn Convent.

The Renaissance Style was introduced into sacral Buildings by the Jesuits in the complex of the Old Town College during the construction of the Church of St. Saviour and the Italian Chapel, and that Style also showed its influence in the interiors of further sacral buildings, such as the Cathedral of Our Lady Before Týn.

In 1611 during the foray of the Passau Troops the Old Town defenders distinguished themselves in the defense against the troops of Colonel Ramée, with whose help Emperor Rudolph II, at the close of its reign, tried to change its unfavorable position against the Czech Estates and his brother Matthias.

Also in the further years the Town was a scene of a number of dramatic events. In 1618 also the Old Town burghers joined the Rising against the Habsburgs. Though Prague was the center of all the events, the Praguers themselves were on the outskirts of the events. In spite of having joined the Rising, Praguers succeeded in the assertion of not all of their requirements with the leaders of the Noblemen's Estates.

The short reign of Frederick of the Palatinate ended with the White Mountain defeat, and it was nothing else than natural that the burghers, though their influence upon the run of the events was petty, again paid for their participation in the Rising more than the noblemen. Fifteen burghers of the Towns of Prague were finally executed on June 21, 1621. A number of burghers had to leave the country, and possessions of other burghers were confiscated or they were fined. When in 1628 non–Catholics left Prague under a degree commanding so, merely Catholics stayed and converts, who changed their belief for a vista of an opportunity of existence. And therefore, when for a short time during the invasion of the Saxony Troops some exiles came back, they were not welcome in the Town.

Prague showed the change of situation in the Town and devotion to the Habsburgs during the siege of the Town by the Swedes, when burghers from the Old and New Towns, together with a small garrison of Emperor's Troops and almost without any cannon, had defended the mean Walls. The resolute resistance of Praguers to the Swedes was evaluated even by the Vienna Court; however, little changed in the political insignificance of the Towns of Prague.

uilding activities revived in the Town soon after the end of the Thirty Years' War. From the mid–17th century the noblemen's Palaces, in the new, Baroque style, began to grow also in the Old Town. The then projects which in particular are worth mentioning are the reconstruction of the Church of St. James in the Old Town, the reconstruction of the Church of Saints Gall, Simon and Judah connected with the establishment of the Convent and Hospital, the construction of the large Jesuit College and of further sacral buildings with which the Baroque was asserting itself in the Old Town in that period until the beginning of the second half of the 18th century. The outstanding constructors of the Prague Baroque, Architects C. Dienzenhofer, G. I. Dienzenhofer, F. M. Kaňka, or J. B. Mathey, C. Lurago, J. Santini, or J. B. Fischer of Erlach, G. B. Alliprandi, J. J. Hrdlička and others, entered through the great secular and sacral building works the history of the Town. Baroque sculpture and painting also are paramount as presented by M. B. Braun, F. M. Brokof, J. J. Bendl, J. O. Mayer, M. V. Jäckel, W. R. Reiner, I. F. Platzer and F. X. Balek, whose works completed the Baroque structures in their exterior or interior. Moreover to the structure of Clam–Gallas Palace on present–day Hus Lane or the splendid Baroque Church of St. Nicholas on the Old Town Square or the Jesuit College, the renowned constructors participated in the construction of new burgher houses, however there the new style asserted itself merely on the frontages and the old layouts of that houses stayed unchanged.

The liking of that period for plastic decor shows in the enrichment of numerous portals and in the installation of the house signs, for instance on Charles Lane, Celetná Street or Rytířská Street. In 1683–1714, thirty statues were installed on Stone (Charles) Bridge, the works mostly by M. B. Braun, F. M. Brokof or J. O. Mayer.

fter the mid–18th century the land coverage in the Old Town was also influenced by the Rococo style, which left there the redecorated frontages on several palaces of noblemen, for instance on the Late Baroque Palace of Goltz––Kinsky on the Old Town Square or also on many burgher houses. Soon however did the Rococo style begin to get out of the way for Classicism, the style of austere shapes and austere decor, whose typical representatives in the Old Town are for instance the Estates Theater (Stavovské divadlo), built at the expense of Francis Anthony Count Nostic.

In the second half of the 19th century applied were as the most frequent the historicizing styles, which imitate first of all the Romanesque, Gothic or Renaissance, and later also the Baroque or Classicism. The ringlet between the Old and the New Town, composed of the present–day streets Národní, Příkopy and Revoluční, was fully covered with new buildings, and the part of the city adjacent to the Vltava's bend was changed due to the clearance. The architectural styles of the second half of the 19th century as well as Sezession art influenced the construction of full blocks of houses on certain streets in the Old Town, such as Paris Street (Pařížská třída). A number of interesting houses are in Sezession style; the Municipal Halls House (Obecní dům) from the beginning of the 20th century, which stands next to the Powder Tower, is particularly prominent.

The Old Town of Prague is a permanent pointer to the eventful history of both Prague and the whole of Bohemia till present days. Its present–day appearence is a result of complex urbanization process from the Romanesque beginnings till the recent past. And the Old Town Quarter also was the center of events at all stages of the Czech history.

The Renaissance portal of the house "At the Two Golden
Bears" (U dvou zlatých medvědů) in Kožná Lane (Kožná
ulička) in the Old Town

67

The Old–New Synagogue (Staronová synagóga) with its high brick–gable is from the period after 1270. The Jewish Town Hall, built in the Late Baroque style, with the Baroque spire and Hebrew clock has its nucleus from the end of the 16th century

68

THE JEWISH TOWN OF PRAGUE

Amongst the inhabitants settled in Prague, from the ancient times the foremost positions in trading have been taken by Jews. On how they moved in Bohemia or neighboring countries, nothing reads, as that occurred undoubtedly in the very old times. They were in this country perhaps in the times of the Markoman tribe, amongst other traders who were coming from the Roman Empire, and they could also be found amongst Czechs in the pagan times and then they enjoyed more respect here …

FROM THE HISTORY OF THE CITY OF PRAGUE
BY WENCESLAS VLADIVOJ TOMEK

The Jewish element in the population of medieval Prague was clear–cut from the very beginnings of urban settlement. Beside Jerusalem also Prague took an extraordinary place in the Jewish tradition. A legend tells the Jews arrived in Prague immediately after the pulling down of the Cathedral of Jerusalem; however, the trustworthy sources indicate that Jews have been settling in the area below Prague Castle as early as in the 10th century. Prague with its Castle in the vicinity of the River, and with a number of smaller settlements running marketplaces and housing traders, was the place where the Jewish traders and immigrants were heading for from two directions. The Jews of Byzantine origin settled around the present–day street Dušní ulice. Some time later Jews arrived on the territory of the Old Town of Prague from the west, and they founded their town there, later called the Ghetto, and that town represented, already in the 11th and 12th centuries, a continuous settlement in the area of the later Jewish Town of Prague, roughly in the place of the present–day streets Kaprova and Pařížská,

towards the bank of the Vltava. When the Old Town of Prague was constituted at the beginning of the second third of the 13th century, the status of the Jewish community was also legislated. The Community was separated from the Christian portion of the city with Walls whose Gateways were locked up by night.

69

the Turks and to cover representation outlays, building activities of the Imperial Court, or political ambitions in the framework of the Holy Roman Empire, and they therefore opened the larger and larger accounts with the Jewish bankers and usurers.

The most important of the Jewish bankers was the unbelievably rich Mordecai Maisel, who often lent considerable sums to Emperor Rudolph II. Maisel succeeded in making full use of the situation, to make the life of his fellow––believers at least partially easier, and therefore he obtained from the Emperor his confirming of old and granting new privileges, which could strengthen the legal safety of the Prague Jews. Maisel was the Primate of the Jewish Community, and his large–scale building activities have influenced the appearance of the Ghetto up to now. Maisel erected the Jewish Town Council Hall (whose present–day appearance dates from the Late Baroque reconstruction) and the High Synagogue in its close vicinity. Maisel also established the originally private Maisel Synagogue, whose present–day appearance is a result of reconstructions after fire and clearance. Visitors may admire the permanent exhibition of "Synagogal Silver" installed in the Synagogue. Maisel, the well–known man, together with his friend Judah Loew ben Bezalel, the learned Rabbi, also established the Talmudic School and took care of the development of Renaissance sciences. Loew became a legendary character of Rudolphine Prague, as by legend he is the creator of the clay figure, say an old version of a modern robot, who was called Golem and had a fantastic bodily strength. Golem's strength could be enlivened with a magic shibboleth on a tangible carrier inserted into a slot in Golem's forehead.

Another personality of the Renaissance Prague, that time ill–fated, was Jacob Bassevi, the banker whose enormous wealthiness came probably from the financial transactions connected with the arming of Imperial Armies and with the speculations with the so–called "light coin" or with the confiscated possessions, he participated in those transactions after the defeat of the Estates Rising together with Albert of Wallenstein and several more noblemen and bankers.

J ews had their internal self–government, however like elsewhere in Europe their status was legalized through the much diversified decrees and privileges in accordance with whether they enjoyed or did not enjoy the protection by the King. Jews were considered as direct subjects, that is, the property of the King, and the King could treat them freely as he liked, for instance he may even have promised his creditors to indemnify them on the occasion of a further pogrom. Though the pogroms were not as frequent as in other countries, they were as cruel as elsewhere. Various events could serve as pretexts for pogroms, for instance the movement of the Troops of Crusade through the city, famine in the country, an epidemy, or incitations by fanatical preachers.

In spite of the lost monopoly on finance and the various limitations, a relative peace was won by the Jewish Community in the second half of the 16th century. The Habsburg rulers needed more and more money to wage wars with

he tombstones of the mentioned persons can be found in the Old Jewish Cemetery (Starý židovský hřbitov) among 12 000 tombstones and tombs from 1439 – 1787. There is also in the Old Jewish Cemetery a collection of Gothic flat tombstones from the 14th century, which were brought in the Cemetery after they had been found during construction work activities on the site of the original Jewish cemetery in the New Town of Prague. The oldest tombstone in the Old Jewish Cemetery is the tombstone of Avigdor Kara from 1439. The Cemetery, whose site size has been kept almost full, is one of the most comprehensive Jewish cemeteries at all and therefore it is a valuable source for learning about the history of Prague Jewish Community.

The entire Jewish population was expelled from the country for two times, in 1541 and in 1744. Those ill–judged decisions each time showed unfavorably in the status of trade and finance, and therefore those decisions were recalled under the pressure of not only the Jews but also Prague burghers and even also noblemen. Each time the Jews incorporated anew into economy of Prague and the whole of the land, however their status did not changed. And it was nothing earlier than the reforms to the spirit of the enlightened absolutism of Joseph II, the reforms through which Joseph II created the prerequisites of the economic prosperity, the prerequisites which substantially influenced the life and government in the Ghetto and lifted the curtain of isolation behind which the Jews had to live. Ten thousand's population were crowded on the territory of several present–day apartment houses, though since 1796 the Jews have been allowed to live even in some houses in the Old Town. Finally in the 19th century the progressive liberalization reforms basically removed the insulation. Recognizable differentiation began to show inside the Jewish Community and many Jews through marriages or everyday common life assimilated with their neighborhood. In most cases the Jews mastered both languages then used in the country, Czech and German, and therefore they inclined, from the language viewpoint, sometimes to the Czech

environment and sometimes to the German environment. A number of successful businessmen–converts got their noblemen's titles.

y the close of the 19th century the area of the Jewish Town of Prague had actually collapsed in social, sanitary and health status aspects. At the beginning of the 20th century the City therefore undertook a large–sized clearance of Medieval, Renaissance and Baroque land coverage on the territory of the Jewish Ghetto and in adjacent parts of the Old Town. This fully removed the flavor of the lanes in the Prague Jewish Ghetto, and together with poor dwellings also a number of buildings were demolished, which should rather have been preserved for the generations to come.

A new quarter of Eclectic and Sezession apartment houses originated on the cleared areas, the apartment houses have become splendid monuments already in the course of this century. From the Old Ghetto only a handful of buildings have remained, mostly Synagogues with the old Jewish Town Hall; the street communication system was partially respected.

The clearance has further speeded up the New Age process of integration of Prague Jews with the cultural, scientific and public life. Their contribution showed impressively in both Czech environment and the German minority until the Second World War, the contribution is symbolized by the names of Franz Kafka, Oskar Baum, Max Brod, Rudolf Fuchs, Jiří Orten and many others.

The thousand–year symbiosis was interrupted by Nazism. The mass–scale emigration and later the holocaust decimated the remaining Jews, who did not have an occasion or means to leave their home or who simply were reluctant to leave. After the War few refugees returned for ever, from the fear of the future development of events. In the following years the rows of emigrants were enlarged by a number of those who had survived the Nazi hell of terror. A large number of citizens of Jewish origin became the victims of artificially constructed allegations and "law" suits in the fifties. A number of them withstood however, and their share in the cultural life of the City and the entire country and in the development of science and technology forms a continuity with the historical tradition and much outnumbers the restricted count of the present–day Jewish community.

he most precious monument of the former Medieval Ghetto is the Old–New Synagogue (Staronová synagóga), one of the oldest and beatiful Gothic structures in Prague. The Early Gothic structure from around 1270 is a two–nave hall with ribbed vaulting supported on two pillars standing in the middle. Outside the Synagogue has brick gables (from the 14th century) and, down, the surrounding annexes. The north annex, for women, dates from the 18th century. The dual nave can be entered through the original portal with plantlike ornaments. Inside the Synagogue located is the Banner from the mid–17th century, which Jews were presented with by Ferdinand III for their help during the defence of Prague against the Swedes. At the east side is the tabernacle with the Renaissance columns, over which is the original Early Gothic fronton, filled in with the vegetable leafage of the tympan.

On the south rim of the Cemetery and the Široká Street stands the Pinkas Synagogue (Pinkasova synagóga), founded in 1479 by Rabbi Pinkas. The Synagogue has a Late Gothic hall, vaulted with the rib net on the Renaissance flying buttresses. The south wing and women's gallery, marked on the outside with the composite Late Renaissance windows, were added as annexes at the beginning of the 17th century. The Pinkas Synagogue is also the Monument to Victims of Racial Persecution.

The Jewish Town Hall (radnice), today the seat of: the Federation of the Jewish Religious Communities in Bohemia and Moravia and the Jewish Religious Community in Prague, originated as the reconstruction of the original Maisel Council Hall, built at the end of the 16th century by Architect Pancras Roder. The reconstruction in the style of the Late Baroque was carried out in 1763 by Architect Joseph Schlesinger. On the roof of the Jewish Town Hall is a wooden spire and its clock.

he Jewish Town Hall building is on its lateral side facing the street Pařížská leaned upon by the High Synagogue (Vysoká synagóga, called also Town Hall Synagogue), built after 1577 at the expense of Mordecai Maisel and enlarged in 1691.

On the street U starého hřbitova stands the Klausen Synagogue (Klausová synagóga) from the end of the 17th century, and newly adapted at the end of the last century. The Ceremonial Brotherhood hold their meeting in the neighboring building, which was built in 1906–1908 by plan J. Gerstel.

Also the Jewish State Museum is an important part of the former Ghetto. By the cruel irony of fate the Museum originated in the present appearance from the initiative of Nazis from the confiscated property of Synagogues and Jewish Communities in Bohemia and Moravia. The collection funds of the Jewish State Museum are now a cultural treasury whose importance is worldwide.

Those monuments and the newly revived traffic in the Prague Jewish Town create a peculiar atmosphere of a town (though not walled in) in a City. Visitors from all over the world flow in here to admire the architectural monuments of the Prague Ghetto and to pay tribute to the Jews so persecuted in the past.

The oldest saved synagogue in Central Europe, the Old–New Synagogue (Staronová synagóga) from the last quarter of the 13th century; its erection was influenced by Cistercian Building Lodge

One of the oldest monumetns of Prague – the Rotunda
of the Holy Rood (rotunda sv. Kříže)
on Karolina Světlá Street in the Old Town

Gothic and Romanesque foundations hide below
the Baroque or Classicistic facades of the houses
on Gall Market (Havelské tržiště)

Pictures from the Old Jewish Cemetery (Starý židovský
hřbitov). Left, the parts of Pinkas Synagogue (Pinkasova
synagóga); right, the parts of Klaus Synagogue
(Klausová synagóga)

The Old Town Hall Tower with the Clock, and the Late
Gothic or Renaissance faces of the Hall's
south fronted houses

The Old Town Clock (Staroměstský orloj) with its calendar
dial famous for the Allegory of Months,
and the Astronomical Clock

High above the Old Town Square protrude the slim towers
and facades of the Gothic Cathedral
of Our Lady Before Týn

PRAGA · CAPVT · REGNI

EDIT
RI TVRRITA
RAGAE
RAE SORTIS-
MOLE SVA VT
SCENDVNT
TVRRES
SVPERAS
AGA TVAM
rtinus Cuthen

OMNIA TVR
CONCEDVNT C
NATVRA
QVIDQVID
HIC CENVS
BONVS AER
AD VITEM
INGENIOS
HIC CAESAR
THEMISQVE N
HIC ALIIS S
IN VRB

The Old Town burghers' proudness is expressed
in the inscription "Praga caput regni" over the exquisite,
Renaissance, composite–window (from 1520)
on the second aldermen's–house of the Old Town Hall

82

On the corner of Paris Street (Pařížská třída) and the Old
Town Square stands the Baroque Church of St. Nicholas
(kostel sv. Mikuláše), built in the years 1732 to 1735
from plans designed by G. I. Dienzenhofer

83

Houses on Celetná Street (Celetná ulice) leading from
the Powder Tower to the Old Town Square are decorated
mostly with Rococo or Classicistic facades; however,
the houses' nuclei date from the periods of Gothic
or Romanesque styles

On the corner of Celetná Street and the Fruit Market
(Ovocný trh) stands the house "At the Black Madonna"
(dům "U černé Matky boží") built at the beginning
of the second decade of the 20th century from a design
in Cubist style by architect Joseph Gočár

85

The Gothic Bridge–Tower and the Baroque dome
on the Church of St. Francis (kostel sv. Františka) dominate
the Old Town end of Charles Bridge (Karlův most)

The Old Town Water Tower and the building in the style
of Czech Neo–Renaissance, design by architect A. Wiehl

The towers and domes of the Churches of Saints Clement, Saviour and Francis (kostel sv. Klimenta, sv. Salvatora, sv. Františka) and the Old Town Bridge Tower (Staroměstská mostecká věž) make a frame to the view of the Cathedral of St. Vitus in Prague Castle

LESSER TOWN

After the death of King Wenceslas in the Kingdom
of Bohemia the Throne was accessed to by his son Přemysl,
the mighty and brave, who behaved manly from the very
beginning of his boyhood and who decorated the nobility
of his Kingly mind with the magnificence of his deeds.
In the endeavor for keeping peace for the inhabitants
of His Kingdom, he commenced to Wall in the towns and
to fortify the Castles. And also, he fortified the Lesser Town
of Prague with Walls and Moats.

FROM FRANCIS OF PRAGUE CHRONICLE

The Lesser Town belongs to the parts of Prague which are the most impressive. No one of the visitors of Prague will forget the views from the Old Town Mills over the River at the Lesser Town Tower Bridges and the stately Dome of the Cathedral of St. Nicholas, at the slim Tower of the Church of St. Thomas and the Church of Our Lady Victorious below Petřín, or at the Palaces and Gardens which climb up to the buildings of Prague Castle and onto the slopes below Strahov Monastery and below Petřín.

The Lesser Town is a whole from a standpoint of urban planners, where not only the eye of the expert, but also the eye of ordinary, a little bit perceiving walker can mention the inseparable and rare symbiosis between the dif-

The house sign of the house called "At the Golden Sun" (U zlatého slunce) on Wallenstein Street (Valdštejnská ulice), from 1623

The statuary of St. Saviour and Saints Cosmas and Damian
(from 1709) was created by J. O. Mayer at the expense
of the Prague University's Faculty of Medicine

Present–day appearance of the originally Romanesque
Church of Our Lady Below the Chain (kostel Panny Marie
pod řetězem) at the Convent of the Knights of St. John or Maltese Knights is a result of the Gothic reconstruction by the Parler Lodge and the Baroque modifications by Architect
Carlo Lurago

ferent architectural styles. In the appearance of its unity joined are stateliness and intimacy, and the mightiness of the architectural palace or cathedral complexes with the peaceful atmosphere of the Lesser Town's lanes and garden corners. The Lesser Town abounds also in natural elements – either the Vltava and its branch, the Čertovka flowing along Kampa Isle, or the large areas of wild growing vegetation on the slopes of Petřín or cultured vegetation in the gardens of the Palaces. That quarter brings along in its virtues the spiritual development from the Romanesque origin through the Baroque to Classicism, and as well the dynamical pressure between burgher streams and their aristocratic counterparts, between the pomp and simplicity, and between the showy manners and functional ways, and therefore the Quarter is a reminiscence of the many features which have died out on the right Vltava's bank, irretrievably, by clearances which touched also the Lesser Town, though not too much.

The origination and further fortunes of the Lesser Town are closely related to Prague Castle. The archaeological researches show that the origin to the present–day Prague should be found on the left bank of the Vltava below Prague Castle, with that the ancient, settlement in the area roughly between present–day Malostranské Square (Malostranské náměstí) and Prague Castle was in reality probably the first actual Prague below–Castle with its Market Place. Its advantage was the position near to the River, however far enough to escape the floods, and first of all on the main distance-route, which after wading of the Vltava on its shallow ford led approximately through present––day Nerudová Street and Úvoz upwards and further westwards.

In the future area of Lesser Town, however, a number of their communities and villages existed, which later partially vanished, partially were incorporated into the organism of the future Town. Having originated along the natural course of communications and plastic relief of the terrain, the Lesser Town did not form a uniform settlement unit by the end of the Ro-

manesque period. The dynamic development of settlement occurred especially in the 12th century.

For the further development of Prague, the reign of King Vladislav I was important – in his reign the role of the right–bank Prague market place had grown immensely and with respect to the event that the wooden bridge on the Vltava had collapsed during a flood, the King ordered an unknown Italian constructor (perhaps from Milan) to built a new, stone bridge in 1158 – 1172, for the honor of his consort Judith. The bridging of the Vltava with the stone bridge of yellow sandstone, enabling heavy waggons to cross the River, allowed a closer connection between the settlements on both banks of the Vltava. The bridge was beside the bridge on the Danube in Regensburg the only stone bridge in Central Europe and the Chronicler called it the Emperor's Deed rightfully. The Bridge was in service until 1342, when it was destroyed by the then flood, and in the end it was replaced by a new bridge in the reign of Charles IV.

To the left of the Bridge's Lesser Town end, protected probably by two Romanesque Towers guarding the Gate, in 1158 the second King of Bohemia, Vladislav, allotted a large site for the Order of the Knights of Saint John of Jerusalem, to be the Order's beneficiary base and to be used for the erection of the Church of Our Lady Below the Chain (kostel Panny Marie pod řetězem) or also of the Bridge's End. Around 1270 the Church was enlarged by a new, already Gothic presbytery. The Beneficiary Base had its own jurisdiction and, as a special entity, was fortified. The Church was largely reconstructed in the second half of the 14th century in the reign of Charles IV, and also other buildings on the Order's territory were adapted in that time. The Parler narthex of the Cathedral and also the two mighty Gothic Towers reminds of the former important standings of that Order and its Prague seat in Bohemia.

On the north side of the Lesser Town forebridge originated another large complex, the Court of Bishops, the ostentatious buildings and large garden, which remind first of all of the last Bishop of Prague, John IV of Dražice, who spent many years of his life at the Papal

The Castle Steps below the south gardens of Prague Castle
lead from Thun Lane (Thunovská ulice) up to the viewing
point before the Castle)

Meissen Lane (Míšeňská ulice), which connects Dražického
Square (Dražického náměstí) located beneath the higher–rise,
Lesser Town Bridge Tower with the At–the–Lusatian–Semi-
nary Lane (U lužického semináře), is lined with Baroque and
Classicistic burgher houses

Court in Avignon. After his return he ordered to rebuilt the inexpressive seat, however at the beginning of the Hussite Revolution the Palace and the adjacent Garden were burnt down and destroyed. From the entire structure, merely the prismatic, Early Gothic Tower, which shows the coat–of–arms of Nobles of Dražice above its entrance, has remained until now.

Let us however return to the first half of the 13th century. Though the Romanesque settlement below Prague Castle showed its undoubtedly urban traits and was already partially fortified, it was a non–uniform, scattered settlement which could easily get out from under the King's rigid control status. The King, without any doubt, was interested in safety in the below–Castle areas, where the road connecting Prague Castle with the Bridge was located. Wenceslas I towards the close of his life, in 1254, ordered to reinforce the Lesser Town forebridge of Judith's Bridge with building Walls and Bastions to the adjacent Court of Bishops and the Convent of the Knights of St. John of Jerusalem.

And four mere years later, in 1257, his son Přemysl Otakar II, founded programmatically the Town, which could, even for strategic reason, be the substitute for the nonuniform settlement between the Castle and Stone Bridge, and he ordered to fortify the Town in Walls and Moats from three sides; it was merely the side adjacent to the Castle where no Walls were built.

The Town bore its name, the New Town Below Prague Castle, and German Colonists were introduced in the Town. (After Charles IV had founded in 1348 the New Town of Prague on the right bank of the Vltava, calling the New Town Below Prague Castle as the Lesser Town of Prague got into common use, and later, Lesser Quarter or Little Town.) And as early as in 1283 in the middle of the Lesser Town Quarter consecrated was by Bishop Tobias the Parochial Church of the new urban community, St. Nicholas, the predecessor to the now existing, Baroque Church; and simultaneously the complex of the Augustinian Monastery of St. Thomas was originating.

Charles IV enlarged substantially the area of the Lesser Town with adding the large area along the bank of the Vltava south of the Base of

the Knights of St. John, together with the entire, large slope of the hill Petřín. And all that was encircled with the so–called Hunger Wall from 1360 – 1362, whose end was at the southeast corner of Hradčany fortifications and which continued from that place to the west rim of Strahov Monastery and further to the Church of St. Lawrence (kostel sv. Vavřince) and eastwards to the Vltava. The arenaceous– marl Wall is some six meters in height and almost two meters in thickness. The new fortification walled to the Lesser Town the area of the Base of the Knights of St. John of Jerusalem, a large portion of the village Újezd, and villages Nebovidy and Strahov.

t the onset of the Hussite Wars in November 1419, the Lesser Town heavily suffered during the fights between Praguers, who hold the Lesser Town Bridge Towers and the House of the Dukes of Saxony standing nearby, and the Royal Garrison of Prague Castle. The Palace of the Archbishop was completely destroyed at the entrance from the Bridge into Lesser Town, the Town Hall in the middle of the Square was destroyed, and the houses below the Castle and the Lesser Town Churches were burn out. In the spring of 1420, when Praguers prepared to face the siege by the Troops of the Crusade, the land building coverage between the Hussite–held Lesser Town forebridge and the Castle was burnt out and destroyed almost in its entirety, in order that it could not be utilized by the Royal and Aristocracy Troops.

And it was no earlier than in the mid–15th century, when the Lesser Town began to recover from the experienced sufferings. In 1464 the base stone was laid to the new erection of the southern Lesser Town Bridge Tower. The two Towers, the original lower–rise Romanesque Tower and the new Late Gothic Tower, have guarded till now the way from the Bridge to Lesser Town's Mostecká little Street.

On the onset of the Renaissance time the Lesser Town began to flower into unusual beautifulness. However, on July 2, 1541 fire originated in the house called. The house "At the Bastion" on the Lesser Town Square,

being bought, in particular by noblemen, from the burghers all of a sudden having got poor after the fire. In the places of several former burgher houses originated the large foundations of urban palaces and their ample yards and gardens.

The Renaissance style elements had been penetrating into Prague at a very modest pace. However now the Renaissance showed in the new constructions of the noblemen's larger building complexes, growing on the burnt sites. And together with the persecution of the Burghers' Estates after King Ferdinand I had put down the revolt in 1547, that entrepreneurship lead to lowering the influence of the Lesser Town's burghers upon government of their Town. The noble builders applied moreover the right to enter their possessions and properties into the so-called Land Rolls, into the ancient institution dated from the second half of the 13th century and representing the archives of decrees, edicts, findings, orders, treaties and property transactions of the members of the Lands Community, i. e. noblemen. the property entered in the Lands Rolls was not subject to the jurisdiction of the Towns, which in its turn ever more lowered the position of the Burghers Self–Government.

The building activities brought also demographic changes. Building craftsmen from the whole of Bohemia gathered in Prague and the numbers also grew of constructors, bricklayers, stucco workers and further craftsmen coming from the Apennine Peninsula. In this way the numerous Italian colony originated in the Lesser Town, which gradually created their Congregation with the Hospital, Chapel and Cemetery.

urther increase in the building activities and numerous immigration occurred during the last quarter of the 16th century, when Prague became the seat of Emperor Rudolph II. In that time the building activities for instance ran in the area between the Bridge and the streets Mostecká, Lázeňská and Míšeňská (Meissen) Street. After the fires of 1503 and 1541 the Church of St. Thomas was repaired, thoroughly and al-

which spread rapid by the strong wind and hit the shingle roofs of the houses around and the Cathedral of St. Thomas; both sides of present–day Nerudova Street were burning. The fire destroyed the houses built below the Castle and hit also Hradčany. During three hours the fire destroyed two thirds of the Lesser Town's area, and from 211 houses, 133 were burnt down.

The fire had basically decided that instead of complicated reconstructions new construction in the so–called "on the green sod" began in many places. After the largest damages had been removed, gradual urban– planning and architectural–styling changes took place in the Lesser Town. The building activities ran on both the original sites of burgher houses and the large sites which in the Lesser Town were

One of the quiet corners in the Lesser Town gardens

ready in Renaissance style. A number of Renaissance houses grew both on Tomášská street and on present–day Wallenstein Street (Valdštejnská ulice) and Letenská Street, and the Renaissance adaptations touched basically all the premises in the whole of Lesser Town.

Trades and crafts were enlivened, the interest of noblemen in building urban palaces grew higher, as witnessed for instance by the construction of the Palace of the Nobles of Hradec (below the Castle) with the up to now still admired gables. The further buildings which originated in that time were for instance the large Palace of Smiřický's on the Lesser Town Quarter, or the Renaissance houses built on Mostecká little Street, and also Judith's Tower at the end of the Bridge was repaired, its battlement removed and gables and roof substituted instead, and the entire Tower coated with sgraffito plaster.

The Late Renaissance period in the end brought an upsurge in the Town, which got its reflection also in the reconstruction of the Lesser Town Hall in 1617 – 1622 (originally the house of John Tovačovský of Cimburk) by John Campione de Bossi from the design by G. M. Filippi. The Hall stands on the Lesser Town Square opposite to the Church of St. Thomas. The present–day appearance of the Hall is a torso of the original appearance, as at the beginning of the 19th century the original gables and towers were torn down.

Sacral construction towards the close of the 16th century and at the beginning of 17th century, similarly as in other Towns of Prague and throughout the Land, stagnated to a certain extent. The new constructions were associated with the changes in urban population, and the German Lutherans, who settled in the Lesser Town, built in 1611 their own Church on Carmelite Street (Karmelitská ulice), likewise as their fellow– believers built the Church of St. Saviour in the Old Town. After 1624, or in the period of the starting recatholicization in the Land, the Lesser Town Church was given to the Carmelites. The church originally was oriented in the traditional way, altar east, however in the thirties in the 17th century during

the Early Baroque adaptation the presbytery was turned and the Tower and frontage were built. The Church of Our Lady Victorious is renowned all over the world for the waxen statuette of the Prague Child Jesus, the Spanish work from 16th century, which was presented to the Carmelites by Polyxena of Lobkowicz in 1628.

Similarly as the Lesser Town German Lutherans, also the Lesser Town Italian Congregation built at the Hospital (1601) on present––day Vlašská little Street their own and naturally, Catholic, Church (1613) of St. Charles Borromeo (kostel sv. Karla Boromejského). Its Old Town counterpart became the Chapel of the Assumption on present–day Charles Lane, adjacent to the complex of the Jesuit College Clementinum.

The first half of the 17th century brought a chain of sorrows and sufferings to the Town of Prague, and from them in particular to Hradčany and the Lesser Town. At first those Towns were occupied and plundered in February 1611 by the mercenary soldiery of the troops of Archduke Leopold, Bishop of Passau, who was called to the Land by Rudolph II to try to bring Rudolph a favorable turning point in his relations to the rebellious Czech Estates and to Emperor's own brother Matthias, who tried to get the succession to the Czech Throne.

The further plundering of the Lesser Town, in particular in the urban residences of noblemen, was the matter of the Emperor's Troops and League's Troops, who entered Prague after the Battle of the White Mountain and after Frederick of the Palatinate set on his flight and left Prague to their fate. Confiscations and emigrations began, and the Lesser Town depopulated to a large degree. And later, when Prague was occupied for some time by the Saxon Troops under John George Arnim, that did not mean anything else than another wrong which the Lesser Town and other Towns of Prague had to withstand, that time from the mercenaries of the Lutheran Elector of Saxony, John George.

The Swedish Troops penetrated into the Lesser Town in 1648. The Old and New Towns of Prague succeeded, due to the bravery of their defenders, in denying their areas, however Prague Castle, Hradčany and the Lesser Town were thoroughly plundered. therefore soon after the end of the Thirty Years' War the buildup of new fortifications to the best knowledge of the then military science began, to continue till the 18th century, when the Baroque fortifications replaced the original Medieval fortifications and dammed the way to the City for enemies in the places which were easiest to penetrate through.

Few succeeded to cope with the unfavorable events during the Thirty Years' War. One of such men was the Imperial Generalissimo, Albert Wenceslas Eusebius of Wallenstein (Albrecht Václav Eusebius z Valdštejna). Albert of Wallenstein took his extraordinary advantages from both his timely conversion to Catholicism and his timely joining the Habsburg side. He utilized its position "in an excellent way": he profited unscrupulously from the after–White–Mountain confiscations, participated in dubious speculations of the Consortium of Banks which was headed by him, and bore himself as a sovereign magnate and an irreplaceable commander of the Emperor's Armies; he actually could boast of capabilities of military commander, however it was his extraordinarily large economic power which was underlying and which allowed him for instance to provide armament, outfit and equipment for an entire army at his expense. The Duke of Frýdlant collected his immense property; by wealthiness, power and influence he took the first place in the Land, actually ahead of the Emperor who often was nothing else than the coronated servant on Wallenstein's military entrepreneuring.

n 1624 – 1630 the Duke got built in the Lesser Town the large palace complex, which took the area of an entire urban quarter or a small town; for the construction of the complex he bought three houses, three gardens and a brick manufacture. The Palace was built by Andrea Spezza and N. Sebregondi from the scheme by G. B. Pieroni, they were active also in Duke's other, out–of–Prague constructions.

The large complex was being provided with an extraordinary care with rare movables,

tapestries, carpets, paintings, statues and tableware.

When Albert of Wallenstein was murdered in Cheb (a west Bohemian town) in 1634, the necessary confiscation List of outfit of the Palace took many pages. Therefore the List represents a valuable source of information on how the splendid seat of a Renaissance magnate looked like, exceeding in splendor and luxury the residence of many a then King. Paintings by Baccio Bianco on the ceiling of the Knights Hall, showing Albert of Wallenstein as God Mart, or the monumental salla terrena with which the Palace opens into the garden, or originally to a complex of several gardens, they witness to Duke's self–confidence and taste. the sculptures decorating the garden were produced (before 1630) by Adriaen de Vries, formerly Painter at Rudolph II's Court. A collection of casts of several of those sculptures is now located in the garden. The original plastic art works were as spoils carried away by the Swedish Troops and were located in Drottningholm Castle.

It is true that Wallenstein Castle did not make a revolution in arts in the Lesser Town; however, Wallenstein Palace (Valdštejnský palác) infuenced deeply the plans of the Town and commenced the change of the mostly burgher land-coverage in the Lesser Town into a Prague district with splendid Baroque Palaces and Gardens.

In spite of: the unfavorable results of the Estates' Revolt and the wars, the reduction of Estates' rights (the rights of Towns in particular), and descending of Prague to a position inferior with respect to Vienna, the construction of noblemen's Palaces continued especially at the end of the 17th century and in the 18th century. Builders are Emperor's generals and colonels and lower officers too, the members of the survived domestic Catholic houses, and some of the Czech converts. Already after 1623 Paul Michna of Vacínov bought the Palace of Vchynských's, but it was his son Wenceslas who rebuilt the then existing Renaissance Palace into the splendid Baroque Palace. The reconstruction of Michna Palace, who was supervised by

The Early Baroque Nostic Palace on Maltese Square
(Maltézské náměstí) was built for Hartvik Count Nostic by
Architect Francesco Caratti during the second half
of the 17th century

101

Francesco Caratti, was completed in as late as in the first half of the 18th century by John Adolf Duke Schwarzenberg, who bought the Palace.

The suite of Palace Gardens below Prague Castle are splendid. Merely the large Fürstenberg Palace was situated so well as it was possible to combine, when its Garden was being founded, the large flat parterre with the impressive coulisse of the terraces. The sites of other Palaces were substantially narrower and claiming steep the Castle's Slope, and therefore such sites were divided, ingeniously, into the systems of terraces, stairs and gloriettes (i. e. arbors), which united the intimacy of dwelling gardens with the far reaching views of the City.

The Baroque and Rococo Palaces, such as: Nostic Palace, Buquoy Palace, Kaiserstein Palace, Morzinský Palace, the Grand Priory Palace (Velkopřevorský palác), Liechtenstein Palace, and others, with the rich and quite often lavish relief and plastic decorations, the Palaces had quite changed the appearance and flavor of the Lesser Town. In its south side along the Vltava and on Kampa Island behind the Čertovka, the branch on the Vltava, and also on the other side onto the slopes of Petřín and below Prague Castle, it was possible to spread the Residences wider and to encircle them with the suite of Gardens, which have created, even for nowadays, the pronounced element of greenery. The Lesser Town got silent and became a large nostalgic still garden corner of Prague, awakening at a very very slow pace into modern times. An exception to this was the Thun Palace on present–day Sněmovní Street. In 1801 the Palace was bought by the Czech Estates, who got the Palace reconstruct into Assembly Palace. Land Assembly, originally the top body of the Estates Community, organized their meeting there in the second half of the last century, when the Monarchy was gradually built as constitutional and Assembly represented the land body of elected members – until 1918. After the origination of the Czechoslovaki Republic, the Assembly Palace became the seat of the Senate of National Assembly, and at present the Czech National Council has its seat there, adhering to the inscription which completes the decoration of the tympan in the middle of the Palace frontage – Salus

Rei Publicae Lex Esto (Felicity of the State Be the Widest Law).

he building entrepreneuring of the noblemen was followed by the richer burghers after the partial economic boom. an interesting land coverage of mostly burgher houses remained, in spite of the later adaptations, in the area of the present–day square Dražického, on Meissen Street (Míšeňská ulice), on Kampa, and on the streets Prokopská, Lázeňská, Letenská, Tomášská or Mostecká. After 1700 the squares and street areas of the Lesser Town were getting, first of all in its central part, their Baroque and later, Rococo or Classicistic flavors. In many places however the period facade only a coulisse hiding the older concepts, which can be told in the internal layouts of the houses and which often deeply influenced and predefined the period configuration of Frontages.

ith the advent of recatholizing, also sacral construction, which was stimulated first of all by Orders (both the older coming back to the Land and the newly introduced to the Land). In the most vigorous way manifested themselves the Jesuits, who, in 1628, settled at the Parochial Church of St. Nicholas in the middle of Lesser Town Square and who built at St. Nicholas at first the Profession House and in 1672 – 1687, in the place after old land coverage, the huge body of the College, dividing the up to then undivided square into two parts. The original Gothic Cathedral gave way, at the beginning of the 18th century, to the monumental construction of the new Cathedral. In 1701 – 1711 Christopher Dienzenhofer built the remarkably vaulted nave of the new Cathedral, and then his son Gillean Ignatius Dienzenhofer built, in 1737 – 1752, the presbytery with the dome, and the construction of the entire complex was completed by Anselmo Lurago with the high–rise Bell Tower, in 1751 – 1756. The interior of the Cathedral is one of the tops of Prague Baroque, consisting in the organic combination of architecture, plastic art and painting into an illusive whole. The crea-

The front (completed in 1710) of St. Nicholas' Church (kostel sv. Mikuláše) is divided into three waves and decorated with the coat-of-arms of Francis Libstein of Kolowraty and the sculptures of Church Fathers

103

tors of the Cathedral here moreover succeeded to implement the magnificent idea in the absolute harmony with the whole, and therefore the structure, though so dominant, melds in the surroundings.

The other top in the Baroque sacral architecture in the Lesser Town is the Convent Church of St. Thomas, dating originally from the second half of the 13th century. The Church was devastated by the fires in 1419 and 1541 and then each time and to a large extent adapted. However, the fundamental layout of the high–rise three–portion vane remained intact and was respected even by Gillean Ignatius Dienzenhofer during his Baroque modifications in 1724 – 1731. The newly erected vaulting was decorated by Wenceslas Lawrence Reiner with the monumental frescoes, which rank among the most important art works in the Lesser Town. Moreover to the period decoration the Cathedral is furnished with a remarkable collection of movables as well as art works from the original decoration, they show the development of the Prague Baroque and with some of the unique works they touch as back as into the Rudolphine period.

Above Thun–Hohenstein Palace (designed by J. Santini, now the Italian Embassy) on the street Nerudova stands the Church of Our Lady, built in 1691 – 1717 by the Order of the Teatins, in whose construction took part the Prague Baroque Constructors Giovanni B. Santini–Aichl and J. B. Mathey. Using the stair between the Palace and the Church, you can ascend from Nerudova Street onto the Castle Steps below Prague Castle.

The witness to encountering between various structural styles in the Lesser Town is the Church of St. Joseph (kostel sv. Josefa) from 1687 – 1693, built perhaps from the scheme by Donat Ignatius a Jesu of Louvain in the style of the Dutch Baroque, with the frontage divided by half–columns and pilasters and decorated with the statues by Matthias V. Jäckel. The painting of the Holy Family and St. Theresa inside the Cathedral are however the works by the noted painter of the Prague Baroque, Peter Brandl, from the beginning of the 18th century.

Already in the course of the Thirty Years' War and due to Grand Prior Rudolph Duke Colloredo–Walsee and Prior Berbard de Witte, the Maltese Knights began to repair their seat. The Convent Church of Our Lady, actually a mere presbytery which remained from the Medieval Church and was made Baroque by Carlo Lurago in the mid–17th century, was adapted as an impressive intimate room, carefully completed with quality decoration and moables. the main altar–painting, the Battle of Lepanto and the Maltese Knights Adoring Madonna, and the painting Beheading of St. Barbara on the side altar are by Charles Škréta from the mid–17th century. In the 18th century, the buildings of the Convent and the Grand Priory Palace were built on both sides of that Church.

The Lesser Town was in the course of the 19th and 20th centuries saved from the radical changes which deeply touched the City districts on the right bank of the Vltava. At the Hospital "Pod Petřínem" of the Congregation of the Sisters of Mercy was built, in 1855, the Late Classicistic Church of St. Charles Borromeo. Otherwise even in the Lesser Town several building of more importance and burgher houses had grown in the historicizing styles. Since 1891 the traveling for the top of Petřín has been eased with the cable railroad, established on the occasion of the Land Jubilee Exhibition, and on the same occasion erected was also the Viewing Tower rising as high as sixty meters and being a small copy of the Eiffel Tower in Paris. The visitor will not forget to see the Church of St. Lawrence, standing not far, near by the Walls. That structure originally founded as Romanesque was made Baroque to the appearance as now at the expense of the Brotherhood of Prague Cooks from the designs by Gillean Ignatius Dienzenhofer. An interest is being attracted by the so–called Mirror–Maze Pavilion with its mirror aisle, which brings the visitor up to the battlefield of the Praguers against she Swedes on Charles Bridge in 1648.

The walk to the Lesser Town sightseeings by far does not end with this. As every house or Palace with its Garden, still corners and lanes have their own history, written by their owners or creators or inhabitants.

The best known view of Prague – Prague Castle, the Lesser
Town Bridge Towers, and Charles Bridge

On Maltese Square stands the statuary of St. John Baptist
by sculptor Ferdinand Maxmilian Brokof, from 1715.
The corner house with the Classicistic facade on the left
is the Old Post, called after the post office which was
in that place during the years 1622 to 1723

A typical picture from the Lesser Town – the lower–rise,
Romanesque Tower showing signs of Renaissance
modifications, and the higher– rise, Late–Gothic Bridge
Tower, and in between in the backgound is the Cathedral
of St. Nicholas, the structure from the High Baroque

107

The mighty towers of the Church of Our Lady Below the Chain (kostel Panny Marie pod řetězem) date from the Parler stage of Gothic reconstruction

The Renaissance, Baroque and Classicistic burgher houses and palaces create the ostentatious trait of Nerudova Street (Nerudova ulice), which climbs towards Prague Castle and Hradčany

One of the Lesser Town picturesque corners. At the end
of Jánská Lane (Jánská ulice) stands the Baroque house
At the Holy Trinity. Before the Classicistic house
on the right is a statue of St. John Nepomuk

The frontages of Kolowrat Palace and Palffy Palace make
a frame to the vista of Prague Castle from Wallenstein Street
(Valdštejnská ulice)

The Renaissance gables of the former Palace of the Lords of Hradec and the huge dome of the Cathedral of St. Nicholas (chrám sv. Mikuláše) are the dukes on the sea of Prague roofs in this picture

The dome of the Cathedral of St. Nicholas from the inside, with frescoes by F. X. Balko. The inside of the Cathedral is an example of pompousness of the High Baroque in Prague

Frescoes on the vaulting of the Church of St. Thomas (kostel sv. Tomáše) are works by Wenceslas Lawrence Reiner from 1728 to 1730

The waxen statuette of the Prague Infant Jesus (Pražské Jezulátko) is a Spanish work from the end of the 16th century. Polyxena of Lobkowicz presented the Carmelite Order with the statuette in 1628

Salla terrena from 1627, the gem of Wallenstein Palace, opens into the garden with sculptures by sculptor Adriaen de Vries

The garden face of the Palace of Wenceslas Michna of Vacínov ranks among the paramount works of the Prague Baroque. Francesco Caratti is supposed to be the author of this reconstruction

A romantic view of Prague Venice – a branch on the Vltava
River, called Čertovka (i. e. "Where Devils Dwell"),
separates Kampa, an island, from the Lesser Town

A bridge–under look, through Charles Bridge, at one
of the Lesser Town Mills on the Čertovka

The slim tower of the Convent Church of St. Thomas
dominates part of the Lesser Town below Prague Castle

THE NEW TOWN OF PRAGUE

**In the year of our Lord 1348, on the day of Saint Marcus,
Charles the King of the Romans and of Bohemia laid
the base stone and founded the New Town of Prague and
ordered to erect the very strong Walls and their Gateways
and very, very tall Towers, from Vyšehrad to Poříč. He also
ordered to plant the gardens and vineyards around the city
of Prague, and for those gardens and vineyards population
increased very much.**

FROM THE CHRONICLE OF BOHEMIA BY PŘIBÍK
OF RADENÍN, CALLED PULKAVA

The new municipal district was allotted the open behind the Walls of the Old Town in a wide elbow–like area between Vyšehrad on the south side and the bank of the Vltava opposite to Štvanice Isle on the north side. The Walls of the New Town of Prague to the length of nearly three and a half kilometers were erected within two years, and on the south side they met the Stronghold of Vyšehrad above the Botič Stream. As the retained portion of the New Town Walls above the Valley of Nusle (Nuselské údolí) say, the Wall was two to three meters in thickness and up to six meters in height and had its walk for defenders. Simple Walls without auxiliary forewalls were protected by moats and ramparts. Two more, large corner–Walls were strengtheners, one of them was at Karlov above the Botič Valley, the other was at the northeast end of the Walls opposite to the Vítkov Hill, and the further strengtheners were nineteen line Towers and three Gates on the carriage–way between two Towers and through the Gate–Fort at St. John, the so–called St. John's or also Blind or also Swine. The New Town was not completely walled in opposite the full length of the Old Town or Vyšehrad. As not walled in stayed also the riverside of the newly founded Town, along the Vltava from the place where the Botič joins the Vltava, Podskalí, up to the rock at St. Wenceslas on Zderaz, where at a later time Charles' son, Wenceslas IV ordered to build the little

121

The New Town Hall (Novoměstská radnice) on Charles
Square (Karlovo náměstí, formerly the Cattle Market i. e. Do-
bytčí trh) is a building from the Gothic and Renaissance times

Castle from which it was possible to watch over the endangered bank. North of that place up to the Old Town Walls a free access to the River was difficult, as a system of weirs formed basically a component in the defence of the unfortified bank. Also the lower part of the New Town along the Vltava was not protected, however to cross the River could hardly be done freely by enemies, with respect to the weirs which joined directly the ends of the Walls Strip on the Vltava bank, and as well going down the headlands to reach the Vltava on the opposite bank could be difficult with respect to the steep slopes existing there.

The urban development plan for the New Town of Prague was developed by an unknown Architect, of course behind such a splendid work the political and spiritual manuscript of Charles IV the Personage can be seen, as his idea of the Residential City which should correspond with the importance of the whole of the Holy Roman Empire formed in the substantially more advanced French and North Italian environments, which were being met closely by him as a young Prince. It is therefore understandable that the then existing Prague conurbation, whose largeness and architectural richness stayed much behind the Charles' requirements of representativeness for the Residence of the most powerful ruler in the then Christendom.

Charles' urban planning concept for the new municipal district considered to cover land in and populate a vaste area of the urban–type settlement, with a multitude of squares, streets, churches and convents, in such a way that Prague could be, at least, comparable with those large cities which he as young Prince could met. Altogether the area of some 360 hectares was included into and individually site divided in the new urban district development land. The three central opens, the Cattle Market (Charles Square–Karlovo náměstí now), which due to its area in excess of eight hestares was then the Europe's largest quarter, the Horse Market (Wenceslas Square–Václavské náměstí now) with its more than four hectares, and the Hay Market

(Senovážné náměstí) as the main square in the Lower Town where hay and cereals were marketed, it was the Town's three centerlines which the network of streets and lanes was related to and oriented towards.

The New Town of Prague should adhere to the same legal statutes as the Old Town did, and should have its independent Town Council. Each who got a necessary site should have begun to erect his house within one month and to complete the construction within eighteen months. It was not allowed to burden the burgher houses with mortgage in excess of half of their values, reason being that the owners of the houses were always able to provide necessary maintenance. Charles in the Deed of Foundation mentioned also the Clause of Special Protection For Jews.

Fenced in the New Town Walls were also the original urban settlements with Parochial Churches and further Parochial Districts, parishes, originated there around the new Churches, so that in the end the New Town was divided into twelve parishes. Moreover to the Parochial Churches Charles himself founded further churches and convents. So after 1362 the Church of St. Apollinaris (kostel sv. Apolináře) began to grow on the Windy Hill in the upper part of the Town, and not far from that place already in 1354 Charles IV founded, for the Order of the Augustinian Nuns, the Convent and its Church of St. Catherine (kostel sv. Kateřiny). From the original Church merely the slim, octagonal at its highest stories, Tower remained until now. For its appearance the Tower is called the Prague Minaret.

In the new large Monastery "na Slovanech" with the Church of Our Lady and the Slavonic Patron Saints (kostel Panny Marie a slovanských patronů) seated was the Convent of the Benedictines (of the Slavonic Liturgy), reminding of the ancient Constantine and Method's tradition and the role of Church in Christianizing Moravia and Bohemia. The construction of the entire complex was commenced in 1348 and completed in 1372 by the Ceremonial Consecration. The monastery was later also called Emmaus.

The newly erected Convent Church of the Assumption and St. Charles the Great (kostel

Nanebevzetí Panny Marie a sv. Karla Velikého) at the highest point of the new urban area above the Botič Valley and opposite to Vyšehrad belonged to the Augustinian Canons and is nothing else than confirming the relation of Charles IV to Charlemagne, whom he proclaimed his predecessor and example to be followed. The stately look of that work is evidenced in particular by the prospect (woodcut) of Prague from 1562.

And also the further Convents which were being founded evidenced the Ruler's integration endeavor, as those Convents were occupied mostly by the friars who had newly come. For instance in the Botič Valley near by the New Town Walls below Vyšehrad the Order of Servites got their Convent with the little Church of Our Lady on the Lawn (kostel Panny Marie Na trávníčku), built after 1360. Near by the Old Town Walls' moat, the huge constructions grew of: the Church of Our Lady of the Snows (kostel Panny Marie Sněžné), belonging to the Carmelites, and the Church of St. Ambrose with the Convent of the Benedictines of the Milan Liturgy (the structure was located in the place opposite to the present–day Powder Tower).

The foundation of the New Town lead also to the reconstruction of the old Dominican Church of St. Clement (kostel sv. Klimenta) in Peter Quarter. The Church was completed sometime by the close of Charles' reign.

Adaptations changed also the Peter Quarter's Parochial Church of St. Peter (kostel sv. Petra) "na Poříčí" and the churches in Jircháře. Also the Zderaz Quarter's Parochial Church of St. Wenceslas (kostel sv. Václava) "na Zderaze" was being newly built, however the Zderaz Convent was destroyed by the beginning of the Hussite Revolution. Already at the beginning of the building activities in the New Town the construction began of: the Parochial Church of Saints Henry and Cunigund (kostel sv. Jindřicha a sv. Kunhuty) in the vicinity of the Hay Market, and the Parochial Church of St. Stephen (kostel sv. Štěpána). All the constructions prove that in the New Town a new ecclesiastical architecture was born and developed. The mutual trait of the New Town's Churches of Charles' reign was the tendency to create the harmonious interior space and to unify external dimensions with respect to the existing and the expected land coverage.

In the reign of Emperor Charles IV every year always on the first Friday after Easter Day in the middle of the Cattle Market, exposed were the Imperial Relics – "reliquae imperiales" –, kept at first in the Cathedral of St. Vitus, and later at Karlštejn Castle. On that occasion always a large wooden structure was being prepared for the Relics; in that place in the reign of Charles' son Wenceslas IV was built the Chapel of Christ's Body.

Charles IV promised the Old Town burghers in a special binding Deed that no harm should occur to them with the foundation of the New Town; he provided for them a free pass through the city and the safekeeping of two New Town Gateways; he however ordered that some crafts, heavily burdening the densely housed and populated Old Town through noise or odor, be moved. The Emperor tried also to join the Towns of Prague in a single whole and he even implemented that intention of his for a time (from 1367 to 1377), but the unbalanced standing of the two Towns and the mutual grudge, malice and spite between burghers made him restore the status quo.

With the origination and land coverage of the New Town the structure of the inhabitants in medieval Prague changed. While in the Old Town the power overbalance was in the hands of the merchant Patriciate, it was the craftsmen of Czech origin who overruled in the New Town from the beginning, though, attracted by the conveniences and vistas of further development, part of the Old Town burghers of dual tongue came there and also various nevcomers from foreign countries settled there.

It was the conditions in the New Town, both ethnic or of national origination and religious and social, which had allowed that in its early phases the Hussite Movement put on the radical forms there. Under the leadership of a former Premonstratensian priest at Our Lady of the Snows, the Hussite Preacher John Želivský and already with the participation of John Žižka of Trocnov, the so–called First Defenestration of Prague occurred here. After the vain negotiations of Želivský with the anti– Hussite aldermen (who were appointed as Town Leadership by King Wenceslas IV) on the release of the im-

The Church of the Assumption and the Slavonic Patron Saints
(kostel Nanebevzetí Panny Marie a slovanských patronů) was
completed, together with the Monastery for Slavonic Benedictines, in 1372

125

prisoned Hussite leaders, the crowd invaded the New Town Hall (Novoměstská radnice) and the Town Councillors present there were thrown out of the Council Hall's windows down on the lances and halberds (July 30, 1419).

The Rising in the New Town thus defined the beginning of the Hussite Revolution, in which the New Town always were a more radical factor than their older and richer Prague neighbor. The New Town leaned upon the alliance with Žižka, and after his head, with his followers, who adopted the name of Orphans.

Similarly as the Old Town, the New Town of Prague was divided into municipal district, and namely Zderaz, St. Stephen, St. Henry, and St. Peter. The division into districts represented at the same time a basis for militia organization, which proved so much during the period of the Hussite Revolution.

However, the mutual grudge between the two Prague Hussite Towns caused steadily the petty clashes, whose conciliation required the help of country Allies, and in the end the grudge got its top on the eve of the Battle of Lipany in 1434, when the Old Town burghers with the support by the Troops of the Noble League abased their permanent rival and destroyed the privileges stored in the New Town Hall.

The Compact of Basel, with which the Hussites obtained the official recognition of their fundamental dogmatic requirements, provided inter alia the equality of rights for Calixtins and Catholics. However, in the Towns of Prague the burghers introduced one more stipulation as a prerequisite for obtaining the burghership, and namely, to take Holy Communion in both kinds. The stone slab with the Compact's clauses was located on the wall in the Chapel of Christ's Body on the largest Market Place in the New Town, and where the Hussite Revolution was begun, in this way the victory of the Revolution was symbolically announced. And finally, Sigismund of Luxemburg was recognized as the King of Bohemia and his succession occurred, and in the delegations for Brno and Jihlava, where the conditions of reference were being negotiated through, appointed were also the burghers

of the New Town, whose Town was confirmed the old privileges and granted new priviliges by Sigismund within his short reign.

In the interregnum, George of Poděbrady got Prague under his control in 1448, after he and his people had penetrated Prague across Vyšehrad and through the New Town Walls (near by Karlov in the Botič Valley). As Regent to the Kingdom and later King of Bohemia, George of Poděbrady leaned upon the Towns. During his regency the New Town burghers erected their new, high–rise prismatic Town Hall's Tower with its Gateway. In the reign of the Jagiello dynasty the building adaptations to the New Town Hall continued, and were at their upsurge during 1521 – 1526 with the reconstruction of the entire South Wing, in which interleaved are the Late Gothic and already the Renaissance elements. Also the Corner Tower were adapted, the new, Renaissance windows were installed on the Tower. the reconstruction was carried out by Benedict Ried of Pístov. After the discontinuation of the Large Jewish Cemetery in the New Town in 1478, the area was divided into individual sites, in the reign of Vladislav Jagiello, and land coverage took place. At least let us mention Vladislav Street, which have up to now existed there. An also until now, near by the National Theatre at the building "Mánes" has stood the Šítkovská Water Tower (Šítkovská vodárenská věž), built in 1489. Water was distributed from the Water Tower in wooden ducts into the fountains in the New Town. Moreover to the erections and reconstructions of burgher houses in that time also the building work activities continued in the ecclesiastical structures: in the reign of Vladislav the abandoned Church "Na Karlově" was repaired and the vaulting in the presbytery restored, building care was devoted also to the little Church of Our Lady on the Lawn, which was damaged during the siege of Vyšehrad in the Hussite Wars. The erection of the freely standing Gothic Bell Tower began in the seventies of the 15th century.

The political struggle between the cities and the noblemen forced the Old and New Towns unite, for a common resistance to the noblemen. To seporated governments the two Towns returned during the reign of Ferdinand I. The New Town burghers also participated in the Revolt in 1547 and after the failure of the Revolt a number of them were punished.

Charles IV ordered to build the Church the Assumption and
to St. Charles the Great (kostel Nanebevzetí Panny Marie a sv.
Karla Velikého) at the highest point of the New Town, above
the Botič Stream and opposite to Vyšehrad

Municipal government was subordinated to supervision by Royal Magistrates and Royal Administrators. And so the position collapsed of the Towns of Prague, having been built over long years. The defeat of 1547 sentenced the Towns of Prague to political passivity.

And it was no earlier than in the reign of Rudolf that the revival of economic life occurred, and also in the New Town in new burgher constructions appear the influences of the new, Renaissance style. In 1609 the Czech Estates had their Assembly at the New Town Hall, and Rudolph II issued finally the Imperial Charter on Religious Liberty. During the foray of the Passau Troops and the readiness for fighting in the New Town, people attacked the Convents as they saw in them the root of all evil, and so in that time the Convent Church of Our Lady of the Snows and Karlov Convent were badly damaged.

he New Town aldermen already on May 23, 1618 joined the anti––Habsburg Estates' Rising. A number of them also had to pay for that in their lives and possessions after the defeat of the Troops of the Estates in the Battle of the White Mountain, or they had to leave the country. During the Thirty Years' War the Swedish Troops besieged for two times Prague. It showed that the New Town Fortifications, which originated in the middle of the 14th century, had been unable to protect sufficiently the City against the then volume cannon fire, and therefore the fortifications were being improved, without delays and with makeshifts at least. In the following years however the needs necessitated to build the modern Baroque fortifications.

At the first stage of renovation of the City after the peace brought by the Treaty of Westphalia (1648) the influence of the new Baroque style asserted itself first of all due to the building entrepreneurship by the victorius Catholic Church, whose vanguard was the Jesuits, followed later by further Orders. The Jesuits got quite a large building site in the New Town in the upper portion of the Cattle Market (Charles Square - Karlovo náměstí), and so the entire half of the south side of the Square was occupied by the complex of College and Church of St. Ignatius of Loyola (kostel sv. Ignáce), which was built from the scheme by Carlo Lurago in 1652 – 1670 and was: enlarged during the further decades by further architects; and also completed with art decoration and movables. In 1773 in connection with the discontinuation of the Jesuit Order the College were converted into Military Hospital.

In the domain of sacral architecture, moreover to making Baroque of the facades and interiors in some of the older Churches, the new style asserted itself in several outstanding structures by the foremost Masters of Baroque. The Convent of the Elisabethan Nuns (between the present––day Botanical Garden – (Botanická zahrada and Albertov) originated in 1724 – 1732 from the plans by G. I. Dienzenhofer at the expense of Margaret of Wallenstein. A large garden, with its end reaching as far as to below the Windy Hill, belonged to the Convent. At that same time the Elisabethan Nuns established also the Hospital which, with its enlargement in the 19th century, has served its purpose up to the present time.

In 1737 – 1741 the Augistinians erected in the Upper New Town, in the place of a Church destroyed at the Hussite Wars, the new Church of St. Catherine (kostel sv. Kateřiny), and namely from the plan by Architect F. M. Kaňka. The Church represents a consistent High Baroque structure and has become famous for its splendid ceiling paintings (by W. L. Reiner) with stucco decor (by B. Spinetti).

On the corner of present–day Národní Street and Voršilská Street M. A. Canevalle had erected (in 1699 – 1704) the Convent Church consecrated to St. Ursula, whose facade is decorated with plastic art by F. Preiss and J. Kohl. However already earlier, after 1674 the buildings of the Convent grew to be completed by 1722. Another structure, as remarkable as St. Ursula's Convent Church, is the Church of the Holy Trinity (at the Convent of the Trinitarians) consecrated in 1703, which was founded by John Ignatius Putz of Adlerthurn and built from the plans by Architect Octavius Broggio.

The new cult of the Baroque Saint John Nepomuk could not stay, similarly as in other

The Church of Our Lady of the Snows (kostel Panny Marie Sněžné), whose presbytery was consecrated in 1397, is connected with the name of the Hussite preacher John Želivský

Towns, without a new Holy Place. Such a Holy Place in the New Town, south of Charles Square and above the ancient route heading to Vyšehrad, is the Church of St. John Nepomuk "On the Rock" (kostel sv. Jana Nepomuckého na Skalce), which represents a paramount work of dynamically conceived architecture by Gillean I. Dienzenhofer from 1730 – 1739 and whose central structure is upgraded with two front Towers. Its contemporary is the Church of (originally) St. Charles Borromeo with the House of Elderly Priests; now the Church belongs to the Orthodox Church and is consecrated to Saints Constantine and Method (kostel sv. Cyrila a Metoděje). This impressive work of Dienzenhofer's is memorable for modern history for in 1942, after the assassination of R. Heydrich, Deputy Reichsprotektor, in the Church hid the Czechoslovakian paratroopers, who, after the hiding place was disclosed by informing against, fought the Nazi odds and decided to end the uneven fight suicidally, by their own hands.

The Baroque and Rococo have up to now been reminded of by many a remarkable work of burgher house or palace architecture. That architecture shows expressively in its decorativeness and picturesqueness in the street house fronts, which were being completed by further architectural styles for two more centuries. Let us pay our attention to several of the works. One of the early works by Gillean I. Dienzenhofer, from 1720, which is especially interesting, is the Summer Palace "Amerika", now the seat of the Museum of Anthony Dvořák, and the other especially interesting work by the same Architect of the Prague Baroque and from the last period of his activity, is Sylva–Taroucca Palace on the street Na příkopě. On the present–day street Hybernská (which begins before the Powder Tower and leads to Masaryk Railroad Station) stands the Early Baroque Palace of Kinský's (Lidový dům i. e. Popular House), which was built in 1651 – 1657 by John Anthony Duke Losi of Losinthal from the plans by Architect Carlo Lurago.

The structure was Classicistically modified on its outside. The other Palace of Kinský's,

which stands on the other side of the street, is dated from the period around 1700. However, what has left from the Palace after its modernization is merely its Early Baroque portal. Adjacent to the Popular House building is Sweerts––Sporck Palace, the Late Baroque and Classicistic structure.

On Panská Lane between Na příkopě Street and Jindřišská Street and near by the Convent of the Piarists stand: the Baroque Neuberg Palace, built around 1730 by Joseph Francis Neuse; and Kaunic Palace, from 1710 – 1720 and by Architect G. B. Alliprandi.

The Enlightenment and Rationalism period since the end of the 18th century has deeply involved themselves in the history of the Towns. The Abolition of Serfdom by Joseph II's Patent increase the inflow of rural population to Prague, which strengthened the Czech layers in the City. The reforms introduced by the Enligtened Absolutism paved ways for new ideas. The self–confidence and therefore also the accompanying self––consciousness of the Czech burghers grew, and in parallel to this, in opposition to the Vienna's bureaucratic centralism, also the regional patriotism grew in noblemen. In this favorable atmosphere, the Classicism comes into the Prague streets to become the prevalent architectural style.

The Classicism asserted itself expressively just in the New Town, to give way in the end to the romanticizing Historicism, representing a follow––up to the old architectural styles. The undoubtedly interesting Classicistic building, which stands on the corner of Panská Lane and Na příkopě Street, is the Church of the Holy Rood (kostel sv. Kříže) from 1819 – 1824; the interesting buildings are also the Classicistic annex to the Church of Our Lady (the annex stands opposite to the Powder Tower), or the house known under its name as At the Hibernians – U hybernů (from 1808 – 1811); the two structures were built according to the plans by J. Fischer.

The crowning of the long–years endeavors of the Czech Nation and its spiritual representatives became, in 1881, the opening of the newly– built National Theater, the stately cultural Chapel of the Czech Nation. The construction from the scheme by Joseph Zítek and in cooperation with a multitude of Czech artists,

Water was distributed from the Šítkovská Water Tower until 1847 in wooden ducts into the fountains in the New Town. Adjacent is the building called "Mánes", built to the spirit of Constructivism

later called the Generation of the National Theater, burnt down short, however in an unbelievable short period of two years the Theater was opened anew in 1883. The decoration by fine arts, in which participated Painters F. Ženíšek, M. Aleš, J. Mařák, V. Hynais, A. Liebscher, J. Tulka and others, and Sculptors B. Snirch, F. Rous, E. Hallman, L. Šaloun, A. Wagner, J. Štursa, J. V. Myslbek and others, that decoration created for the first time the conditions for a confrontation of the historical tradition with the then existing mental views of the Czech society, and in a number of aspects that decoration was a deed of laying the base stone.

In a similar way the self–confidence of the revived Nation has entered itself into the appearance of the New Town and the whole of Prague by the neo–Renaissance construction of the National Museum (Národní muzeum), then still Museum regni Bohemiae, the work from the scheme by Joseph Schulz ended by 1890 at the upper end of Wenceslas Square. The bringing to the origination of the Nation–Wide Palace, which became the basis for Czech sciences and one of the foremost European collection––and–science institutions, should however be seen in the Patriots Institute, which was founded by a circle of enthusiastic learned amateurs and scientists in 1818.

The dizzying urban–planning upsurge of Prague started with the industrialization process at the beginning of the 19th century. In the place of the green strip of vienyards, orchards and fields, little villages and the groups of suburban houses, grew the new industrial suburbs, at first with textile industries and later with the manufacture of machines. The New Town was touched by the industrialization only indirectly. Though in the New Town still a number of opens or rarely populated areas existed, the industries were satisfied with the opens outside the Town Walls. There still remained reserves for the municipal needs, for the hospital development and later the University houses development in the open areas between Charles Square, Karlov and Vyšehrad.

The remarkable trait is the complex of unplastered brick buildings in the style of the North German Gothic architecture – the Prague Maternity Hospital, which was before located in the former Canon's Residence at St. Apollinaris nearby.

Since 1845, when the first train entered Prague on a route being then newly built in the direction for Olomouc, Brno and Vienna, the New Town became the nucleus for the future Prague railroad node. The building of the first Prague railroad station, Emperor Francis I's Railroad Station (from 1844 – 1845; today's Masaryk Railroad Station), which is a Late Classicistic structure with two Towers (built from the scheme by Anton Jüngling), has remained in full operation up to now. the enlargement in the network or railroad routes necessitated a reconstruction of the Prague railroad node in the eixhties. A new, central Railroad Station of Francis Joseph I (today, Wilson Prague Main Railroad Station) was built and was interconnected with all main railroads, especially after the digging of the tunnel under Vinohrady Quarter in the direction for Tábor, Budějovice and Linz. the building of Francis Joseph's Railroad Station, from 1901 – 1909, is one of the most valuable examples of the Prague Sezession, which together with the neo–Baroque represents the high period in structural eclecticism and the formal looseness in the land development of new Prague.

A parade of structures of outstanding level from the end of the 19th century and from the beginning of the 20th century is offered by Wenceslas Square. For instance the Sezession hotel Evropa from 1906, or the neo–Baroque Palace from 1895 on the corner of Jindřišská Street and Wenceslas Square, or the Wiehl's House from 1895 – 1896 on the corner of Vodičkova Street and Wenceslas Square (with facade and genre–paintings produced to M. Aleš and J. Fanta). If however the visitors are receptive, they can on their walks through the New Town see such gems on every Square and almost in any of the streets in the New Town. The New Town has been getting lovelier even throughout further years, till nowadays. By a strike of good luck the New Town remained in most cases free from ugly large–scale land development, though an unpleasant inroad into its situation and atmosphere was the ill–advised placing of the highway directly in the Town. In spite of that, the New Town with its central Wenceslas Square is the live and livest part of the Capital.

VYŠEHRAD

After the example of the ancient Emperor Constantine, King
Wratislaw carried up twelve baskets of stone on his own
shoulders, laid foundations for the construction, and
ordered to erect the Vyšehrad Church after the example
of St. Peter's Church in Rome. And that was the way
in which King Wratislav, through his keen and capable
mind, abased the arrogant absence of the said brother of his,
Bishop of Prague; and he chose his Vyšehrad Church as
the place for his sepulchre, and he upgraded very much that
Church with both sacral decorations and necessary needs
and possessions. For he also appointed the Provost
of Vyšehrad the Chancellor of the Kingdom and he
arranged cleverly that the Provost might be at King's
councils and sit there among the foremost men
of the Kingdom.

FROM THE CHRONICLE OF BOHEMIA BY PŘIBÍK OF RADENÍN,
CALLED PULKAVA

Dominant in the Vyšehrad Cemetery (vyšehradský hřbitov) is the Slavín – the last reposing place of Czech Nation's personages

134

On the rocky headland falling on its end steep down to the stream of the Vltava stood once the seat of the Kings and Princes of Bohemia. Vyšehrad was founded probably no earlier than in the second half of the 10th century as the other Kingly Castle to guard entrance to the Prague basin. The earliest authentic witness to Vyšehrad is brought by the denarii struck in the Vyšehrad Mint of Boleslav II and his successors. The upsurge however of Vyšehrad Castle occurred in the reign of Prince Wratislaw II (as the first King of Bohemia, Wratislaw I, 1085 – 1092), who transferred his seat from Prague Castle to Vyšehrad. King Wratislaw I founded in Vyšehrad inter alia the Church consecrated to St. Peter and later also to St. Paul, and he also established the Chapter at that Church, independent of the Bishop of Prague and subordinated directly to the Pope.

The provost of Vyšehrad held the post of the Chancellor with the King and also with several more rulers. The importance of the alternative Royal Residence was stressed by Wratislaw I even with the construction of his representative Romanesque stone Palace. The Vyšehrad Coronation Codex of King Wratislaw dates probably from 1085. Vyšehrad, however, had declined in the late 12th century and in the 13th century into a second position in comparison with Prague Castle.

And it was only Charles IV who restored the political and military importance of Vyšehrad. He ordered to reconstruct first of all and with broadmindedness the Royal Palace. Fully to the spirit of military views of that time and in the years 1348 – 1350, the construction was carried out of mighty fortifications of Vyšehrad, with two main Entry Gateways, from which Špička on the south side was a massive carriageway post, well discernible still on the prospects of Prague from the 16th and 17th centuries. One of the important clauses of the Charles' new Kings of Bohemia Coronation Regulations became the stipulation commanding that each would–be King should set on a journey for Vyšehrad on the eve of his coronation. Charles IV formulated the position of Vyšehrad, it can be said, in a constitutional and legal form, when he had installed in the Kings of Bohemia Coronation Regulations the clause that the Coronation Ceremony should be commenced in Vyšehrad

Castle, where permanently kept should be Přemysl the Ploughman's bag and bast shoes, the assumed relics commemorating the moment when the Ploughman was called from his share to the Princely Throne to become the founder of the first domestic dynasty; by the way, also Charles IV came on the mother's side from that dynasty, and he stressed consistently his Czech lineage.

After 1369 the reconstruction of Chapteral Church of Saints Peter and Paul (kostel sv. Petra a Pavla) was commenced. The reconstruction, though supported by the King from the very beginning, lasted till the beginning of the 15th century. Probably the architectural example of the basilicas from southern France was applied during the reconstruction. Moreover to the prolonged reconstruction of the Chapteral Church also the reconstruction of other buildings of Vyšehrad land coverage was begun, first of all on the houses of canons and priests. In 1361 also in Vyšehrad the stone water–supply system was built, which brought water from as distant areas as the present–day Pankrác and Jezerka in Michle Quarter, which in that time was quite a distance from the Walls of Vyšehrad. That project in its entirety was related also to the raising of grapevine on the southern slopes of the Vyšehrad headland and its irrigation requirement, and the inhabitants of Vyšehrad also needed good quality water.

The end to the restored glory of Vyšehrad came at the beginning of the Hussite Revolution. On November 1, 1420 the King Sigismund of Luxemburg's garrison, who were starved by the long siege, surrendered Vyšehrad Castle to the allied Hussite troops. For on that day the successor to the Czech Throne, unrecognized by the Hussites, was put to rout by Praguers and their allies of Tábor, Žatec, Louny, Slaný and the East Bohemia Oreb Union, on the Pankrác Plain before the eyes of the Vyšehrad troops, whom Sigismund tried to give aid with his troops. The Vyšehrad mercenaries kept knightly to the conditions of armistice concluded with the Hussites already before and did not intervene in the battle. Then the Walls of Vyšehrad opposite to the city were torn down in several places and the abandoned Vyšehrad complex was added to the New Town. In the reign of King Vladislav II Jagiello (King 1471–1516) in the last quarter of the 15th century an attempt occurred of founding the Town of Vyšehrad Mountain, however the community composed mostly of small craftsmen lived their nothing else than a pure existence for one and a half centuries, in particular after the restoration of the Chapter's property rights in the 16th century.

Since 1654 after the resolution of Ferdinand III Vyšehrad began to change in a mighty Baroque Citadel in connection with the renewal of Prague fortifications, which showed as obsolete and mean during the Thirty Years' War. Moreover it only was proven that Vyšehrad played a key role in the then campaigns advancing towards Prague, the role of a fortress guarding entrance to Prague from the south or the south–east. the fortress system was based upon general pentagonal layout with robust corner bastions. The experience of the Italian and Dutch fortification schools was applied throughout the project. Until 1866, when the Citadel was discontinued, merely the Chapter at Saints Peter and Paul survived there in its original function.

In 1883 Vyšehrad together with its below––Castle settlement was raised to the sixth urban district, however the Citadel belonged to Military Administration until 1911.

After the discontinuance of the Citadel the patriotic Canons contributed to a great extent to the revival of the traditional glory of Vyšehrad, that time as a national Cultural Monument. The little Vyšehrad Cemetery (vyšehradský hřbitov) became the last reposing place for the personages of the National Revival, political life and culture, and it has remained for ever as the National Cemetery of the utmost importance; then the fortress area was modified to become the Public Park.

Vyšehrad nowadays is being devoted the comprehensive care, and if the complex terrain and structural conditions allow, Vyšehrad undergoes systematic archaeological researches.

The oldest preserved monument of Vyšehrad reminding of its upsurge in the reign of King

Wratislaw I is the Romanesque Rotunda of St. Martin from the 11th century, standing near by the Leopold Gateway, the second internal gateway of the Baroque fortress, from 1676 – 1678.

The original Romanesque Basilica of Saints Peter and Paul from the end of the 11th century was much enlarged already at the beginning of the 12th century and than it was modified in the Early Gothic style after the half of the 13th century. The Cathedral was completely rebuilt and superbly decorated in the reign of Charles IV, however after the fall of Vyšehrad in November 1420 serious damages occurred. After the restoration of the Chapter the Cathedral was again renewed in the 16th century and at the beginning of the 17th century, and during the first half of the 18th century, the creators of the Prague Baroque J. B. Santini, F. M. Kaňka and G. A. Canevalle participate to a different extent in the Baroque reconstruction of the Cathedral. The present– day appearance of the Cathedral is the result of the reGothicizing which was carried out at the end of the 19th century and at the beginning of the 20th century under Joseph Mocker. Nowadays this Monument is undergoing a large reconstruction.

The Cemetery whose dominant is Slavín, the monumental crypt from the end of the 19th century, is the last reposing place for the personages of Czech art, science and culture of the 19th and 20th centuries. It is possible to find there the tombstones of many giants often of European or world importance, and to see there a number of works of funeral plastic art and architecture. The Cemetery is considered as a unique, architecturally balanced entity, memorable for the Czech national past as well as present.

Quite unforgettable is for Vyšehrad visitors the view, from the fortress corner above the Vyšehrad Rock, of Prague Castle, the city below it, and the Vltava with its bridges.

The Monument (by sculptor J. V. Myslbek) to St. Wenceslas,
the Patron of Bohemia, on Wenceslas Square
(Václavské náměstí)

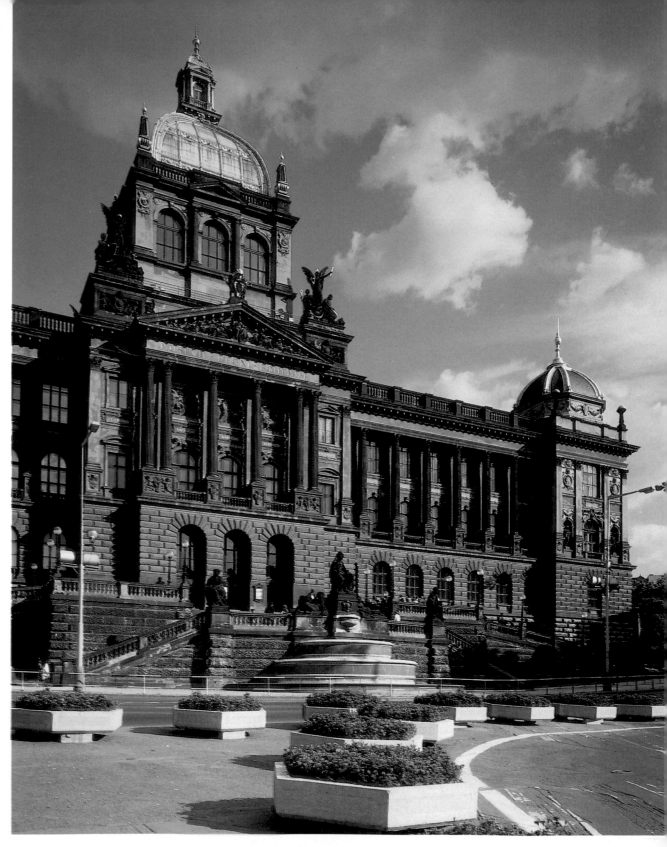

The frontage of the National Museum (Národní muzeum)
built in Neo–Renaissance style in 1885 – 1890 from plans
prepared by architect Joseph Schulz; the Museum dominates
Wenceslas Square

The entrance Hall of Columns in the National Museum.
Below the glass ceiling, placed are 16 busts of the men,
who made their best to establish the Museum

The Monument ot Joseph Jungmann, the writer and
a distinguished representative of the National Revival.
The square which bears his name is located very close
to Wenceslas Square

Two houses on the corner of 28th October Street (ulice 28. října) are compatible in a very rare manner, though built during the periods of different architectural styles

Originally a Romanesque basilica consecrated to St. Peter
in "On the Riverside" quarter (na Poříčí); the basilica
underwent several Gothic modifications, from which the last
one was performed by architect Joseph Mocker towards
the close of the 19th century

The altar picture in the Church of St. Ignatius (kostel sv.
Ignáce) on Charles Square is the work by painter
J. J. Heinsch from 1677; the picture is located in the altar
which is conceived as Classicistic

143

The oldest preserved monument in the New Town
on At the Pond Street (ulice Na rybníčku) is the Rotunda
of St. Longinus (rotunda sv. Longina) from the beginning
of the 12th century

The summer house of Wenceslas Michna of Vacínov,
also called America, is a work by the Prague Baroque
architect G. I. Dienzenhofer

146

The gentle Baroque structure by G. I. Dienzenhofer
is the Church of Saints Cyril and Method (kostel sv. Cyrila
a Metoděje), originally the Church of St. Charles Borromeo
on Ressl Street (Resslova ulice), which connects Charles
Square with the embankment of the Vltava River

Front of the tower of the Baroque Church of St. John
Nepomuk "on the Rock" (kostel sv. Jana Nepomuckého
na Skalce), built during the years 1730 to 1739 from a design
by G. I. Dienzenhofer

147

148

The Parochial Church of Saints Henry and Cunigund
(kostel sv. Jindřicha a sv. Kunhuty) on Jindřišská Street
dates from the second half of the 14th century,
the Renaissance vestibule (narthex) was added around 1525.
The reGothicizing of the Church was performed by architect
Joseph Mocker during the period of 1875 to 1889

Arcades along the inner circumference of the Vyšehrad
Cemetery (vyšehradský hřbitov) are a work by architect
Anton Wiehl during 1889 – 1893

The Leopold Gateway, the internal entrance to the Vyšehrad Stronghold was built in the years 1676 to 1678 from a design by Carlo Lurago

One of the traditional Prague vistas – the Vyšehrad Rock with the remnants of Gothic fortifications from the time of Charles IV, and the slim towers of the Neo–Gothic Church of Saints Peter and Paul (kostel sv. Petra a Pavla)

Prague

A WALK THROUGH HISTORY

THE CONCEPT AND TEXT:
Marie Vitochová
and
Jindřich Kejř

Photographs:
Jiří and Ivan Doležal

Cover and Graphical Layout:
Václav Rytina

Translation:
Ladislav Cífka, M. Sc.
First Issue, Prague 1992

Published by:
V RÁJI Publishing House,
as its 3rd publication,
152 pages

Responsible Editor:
Kateřina Vitochová

Printed by:
Tiskárny Pardubice

The tower of the little Church of the Annunciation
of Our Lady (kostelík Zvěstování Panny Marie)
below Vyšehrad, from the period after 1360